# Raspberry Pi Essentials

Get up and running with the Raspberry Pi to develop captivating projects

**Jack Creasey**

**[PACKT] open source**\*
PUBLISHING   community experience distilled

BIRMINGHAM - MUMBAI

# Raspberry Pi Essentials

First published: April 2015

Production reference: 1230415

Published by Packt Publishing Ltd.
Livery Place
35 Livery Street
Birmingham B3 2PB, UK.

ISBN 978-1-78439-639-8

www.packtpub.com

# Credits

**Author**
Jack Creasey

**Reviewers**
P Ashwin
Scott Gibson
Yegor Yefremov
Werner Ziegelwanger

**Commissioning Editor**
Julian Ursell

**Acquisition Editor**
Sonali Vernekar

**Content Development Editor**
Siddhesh Salvi

**Technical Editor**
Rohith Rajan

**Copy Editor**
Sarang Chari

**Project Coordinator**
Nidhi Joshi

**Proofreaders**
Safis Editing
Paul Hindle
Kevin McGowan
Dan McMahon

**Indexer**
Tejal Soni

**Graphics**
Sheetal Aute

**Production Coordinator**
Aparna Bhagat

**Cover Work**
Aparna Bhagat

# About the Author

**Jack Creasey** has been in the technology industry for more than 30 years, the last 15 years as a Senior Program Manager in hardware and software design. His expertise includes designing, developing, and teaching IT courseware. He is an avid inventor and holds 13 patents in hardware and software design.

After retiring early from the computing industry, Jack avidly participates in social network groups that share his passion for next generation technology solutions.

# About the Reviewers

**P Ashwin** is a Bangalore-based engineer who wears many different hats depending on the occasion. He graduated from IIIT Hyderabad in 2012 as a Master of Technology in Computer Science and Engineering. He has a total of 5 years of experience in the software industry where he worked in different domains, such as testing, data warehousing, replication, and automation. He is very well versed in DB concepts, SQL, and scripting with Bash and Python. He has earned professional certifications in products from Oracle, IBM, Informatica, and Teradata. He's also an ISTQB certified Tester.

In his free time, he volunteers for different technical hackathons and social service activities. He was introduced to Raspberry Pi in one of the hackathons and he's been hooked on it ever since. He writes a lot of code in Python, C, C++, and Shell on his Raspberry Pi B+ cluster. He's currently working on creating his own Beowulf cluster of 64 Raspberry Pi 2s.

**Scott Gibson** is an Electrical Engineer from Ottawa, Ontario Canada. He works as a software developer in the wireless telecommunications industry as well as a consultant specializing in embedded hardware and software development.

Scott has a passion for all things technical with particular interest in projects that cross between software, hardware, and mechanical engineering. Scott runs the website `www.thegreatgeekery.com` documenting some of his personal projects as well as contributions to the open source community.

**Werner Ziegelwanger** (MSc) has studied game engineering and simulation and got his master's degree in 2011. His master's thesis was published with the title *Terrain Rendering with Geometry Clipmaps for Games* by *Diplomica Verlag*. His hobbies are programming, games, and all kinds of technical gadgets.

Werner worked as a self-employed programmer for many years and mainly did web projects. At that time, he started his own blog (`http://developer-blog.net`), which is about the Raspberry Pi, Linux, and open source technologies.

Since 2013, Werner has been working as a Magento developer and head of programming at mStage GmbH, an e-commerce company focused on Magento.

# www.PacktPub.com

## Support files, eBooks, discount offers, and more

For support files and downloads related to your book, please visit www.PacktPub.com.

Did you know that Packt offers eBook versions of every book published, with PDF and ePub files available? You can upgrade to the eBook version at www.PacktPub.com and as a print book customer, you are entitled to a discount on the eBook copy. Get in touch with us at service@packtpub.com for more details.

At www.PacktPub.com, you can also read a collection of free technical articles, sign up for a range of free newsletters and receive exclusive discounts and offers on Packt books and eBooks.

https://www2.packtpub.com/books/subscription/packtlib

Do you need instant solutions to your IT questions? PacktLib is Packt's online digital book library. Here, you can search, access, and read Packt's entire library of books.

## Why subscribe?

- Fully searchable across every book published by Packt
- Copy and paste, print, and bookmark content
- On demand and accessible via a web browser

## Free access for Packt account holders

If you have an account with Packt at www.PacktPub.com, you can use this to access PacktLib today and view 9 entirely free books. Simply use your login credentials for immediate access.

*This book is dedicated to my wife, April. Without her dedication and support this book would not exist.*

*April provided encouragement to start the project, and acted as the Instructional designer and editor once underway.*

*Her patience and input as we built the learning objectives helped us meet most of the deadlines, and significantly enhanced the materials.*

*I can only hope she will perform this function again for the next book.*

# Table of Contents

# Preface

The Raspberry Pi is a low-cost, highly capable computer system about the size of a deck of cards that can use a standard-sized keyboard, monitor, and mouse. This book will show you how to use this amazing little machine to design and configure your own development environment, build really cool hobby projects, and gain expertise in project design and development. You will also learn how to take advantage of existing open source tools, applications, and scripts.

It doesn't matter whether you are new to the hobby project world or you are an experienced DIY maker; from the very first chapter, we guide you through complex software and hardware concepts. This book uses a project-based learning design, from setting up a graphical desktop interface to driving a line-following robot; you learn what you need to know when you need it.

As you complete the projects, you will build on what you learn in the chapters and continue to expand your expertise, using complex computing solutions for your Raspberry Pi.

## What this book covers

*Chapter 1, Getting Started with Raspberry Pi*, introduces the features of the Raspberry Pi and its peripherals. You will build your own Raspberry Pi system and configure the base OS.

*Chapter 2, Configuring the Raspberry Pi Desktop and Software*, continues with the configuration of a Raspberry Pi project development environment based on the use of graphical desktop applications. You will build a talking clock using a Raspberry Pi sound card.

*Chapter 3, Raspberry Pi and Cameras*, explores the configuration of the Raspberry Pi to support various video solutions. You will create a camera-based movement detection system with PiCam and USB cameras, using Bash Shell and Python 3 scripts.

*Chapter 4, Raspberry Pi Audio Input and Output,* examines audio capability and the configuration of the Raspberry Pi to support high-quality sound. You will build an Internet radio and stereo audio system using VLC.

*Chapter 5, Port Input and Output on the Raspberry Pi,* explains digital I/O configuration. You will experiment with LEDs as output indicators and sensing switches to make improvements to the Internet radio.

*Chapter 6, Driving I2C Peripherals on the Raspberry Pi,* describes the characteristics of I2C protocols and the extensive I2C interface support built into the Raspberry Pi. You will build an RC servo control program.

*Chapter 7, Going Mobile with Raspberry Pi,* explores wireless access from the command-line to a remote Raspberry Pi and battery power systems. You will configure remote access to a Raspberry Pi.

*Chapter 8, Creating a Raspberry Pi Line-following Robot,* builds upon projects completed in previous chapters to design the architecture for a Raspberry Pi-driven robot. You will construct a line-following robot using PiCam as the line sensor.

# What you need for this book

The content was based on:

- NOOBS Version 1.4.0, released on February 18, 2015
- Raspbian (Debian Wheezy) Version 7.8 (Linux Kernel 3.18), released by RaspberryPi.org on February 16, 2015

For details, visit `http://www.raspberrypi.org/downloads/`.

# Who this book is for

*Raspberry Pi Essentials* is intended for hobbyists and academic project designers and developers who have minimal experience with programming languages and hardware designs. Don't worry if you are new to computing, this book will coach you through cool projects that ensure you build expertise and competence. Since the Raspberry Pi is an inexpensive computing solution, you can easily build a very cost-effective and flexible graphical desktop environment to develop your hobby projects.

# Conventions

In this book, you will find a number of text styles that distinguish between different kinds of information. Here are some examples of these styles and an explanation of their meaning.

Code words in text, database table names, folder names, filenames, file extensions, pathnames, dummy URLs, user input, and Twitter handles are shown as follows: "You will often see the Wi-Fi configuration utility referred to in configuration guides as the wpa_supplicant GUI user interface."

A block of code is set as follows:

```
[Desktop Entry]
Encoding=UTF-8
Type=Application
Name=Screenlock
Name[en_GB]=Screenlock
Icon=kscreensaver
```

When we wish to draw your attention to a particular part of a code block, the relevant lines or items are set in bold:

```
[Desktop Entry]
Encoding=UTF-8
Type=Application
Name=Screenlock
Name[en_GB]=Screenlock
Icon=kscreensaver
```

Any command-line input or output is written as follows:

```
sudo apt-get update
```

**New terms** and **important words** are shown in bold. Words that you see on the screen, for example, in menus or dialog boxes, appear in the text like this: "Clicking the **Next** button moves you to the next screen."

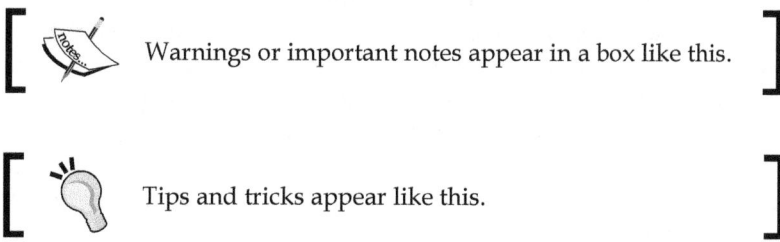

Warnings or important notes appear in a box like this.

Tips and tricks appear like this.

# Reader feedback

Feedback from our readers is always welcome. Let us know what you think about this book—what you liked or disliked. Reader feedback is important for us as it helps us develop titles that you will really get the most out of.

To send us general feedback, simply e-mail `feedback@packtpub.com`, and mention the book's title in the subject of your message.

If there is a topic that you have expertise in and you are interested in either writing or contributing to a book, see our author guide at `www.packtpub.com/authors`.

# Customer support

Now that you are the proud owner of a Packt book, we have a number of things to help you to get the most from your purchase.

# Downloading the example code

You can download the example code files and the supplement chapters for this book, from your account at `http://www.packtpub.com` for all the Packt Publishing books you have purchased. If you purchased this book elsewhere, you can visit `http://www.packtpub.com/support` and register to have the files e-mailed directly to you. The example code files can also downloaded from `http://1drv.ms/1ysAxkl`.

# Downloading the color images of this book

We also provide you with a PDF file that has color images of the screenshots/diagrams used in this book. The color images will help you better understand the changes in the output. You can download this file from `https://www.packtpub.com/sites/default/files/downloads/6398OS_ColorImages.pdf`.

# Errata

Although we have taken every care to ensure the accuracy of our content, mistakes do happen. If you find a mistake in one of our books—maybe a mistake in the text or the code—we would be grateful if you could report this to us. By doing so, you can save other readers from frustration and help us improve subsequent versions of this book. If you find any errata, please report them by visiting `http://www.packtpub.com/submit-errata`, selecting your book, clicking on the **Errata Submission Form** link, and entering the details of your errata. Once your errata are verified, your submission will be accepted and the errata will be uploaded to our website or added to any list of existing errata under the Errata section of that title.

To view the previously submitted errata, go to `https://www.packtpub.com/books/content/support` and enter the name of the book in the search field. The required information will appear under the **Errata** section.

# Piracy

Piracy of copyrighted material on the Internet is an ongoing problem across all media. At Packt, we take the protection of our copyright and licenses very seriously. If you come across any illegal copies of our works in any form on the Internet, please provide us with the location address or website name immediately so that we can pursue a remedy.

Please contact us at `copyright@packtpub.com` with a link to the suspected pirated material.

We appreciate your help in protecting our authors and our ability to bring you valuable content.

# Questions

If you have a problem with any aspect of this book, you can contact us at `questions@packtpub.com`, and we will do our best to address the problem.

# 1
# Getting Started with Raspberry Pi

While there are many operating systems (OS) available for the Raspberry Pi, the Raspberry Pi Foundation (`http://www.raspberrypi.org`) offers Raspbian as the primary OS. Raspbian (`http://www.raspbian.org`) is based on yet another operating system called Debian, which is built on a Linux kernel for the Raspberry Pi.

## Let's get started

The **Raspberry Pi**, or just **Pi** as it's called by project designers, is a complete computer system on a small motherboard. In this chapter, you will learn to manage and use the computer with a simple black box methodology. With this simple methodology you don't need to understand the architecture or the internal working of a computer, but you will need to know how it responds to various input and output methods.

At the top level is user input and output. We will use the Raspbian graphical desktop interface as much as possible to simplify interactions with the computer. At the hardware level, you will need to understand the connectors and their purpose. You need not understand the internal architecture of your Pi to complete a project.

There are various models of the Raspberry Pi, which range from one with 256 MB memory with a single-core ARM CPU through to the latest with 1 GB memory and a quad-core ARM CPU. For all of the projects in this book, you can use any of the Raspberry Pi models (they all run the same Raspbian release) with only a slight difference in the I/O connectors to contend with.

We will ignore the internal Raspberry Pi configuration in this book unless it is required to complete a project. So, you won't need to know the CPU type or memory architecture, but you will need to understand the ports (connections) on the board. We've listed the input and output ports available for the Raspberry Pi A+, Raspberry Pi B+, and Raspberry Pi 2 Model B models:

- **AV I/O**: This is a four-contact 3.5 mm **TRRS** jack that provides composite video and stereo audio output

- **Camera interface**: This is a **mobile industry processor interface** (**MIPI**) and **camera serial interface** (**CSI**) fifteen-pin camera connector that supports the **PiCam** and **Pi NoiR** cameras

- **Ethernet port**: A single RJ45 connector that supports a 10/100-Mbps network connection (the Ethernet controller is connected to the USB bus; there is no Ethernet on the A+ model)

- **GPIO**: This is a forty-pin 0.1" header with 5v, 3.3v, 17 GPIO, UART, I2C, SPI, I2S, and EEProm C/D (some shared pin functions)

- **HDMI port**: A single HDMI connector supporting resolutions up to 1920*1200, along with digital audio

- **LCD interface**: An MIPI (DSI) fifteen-pin LCD connector

- **Micro USB port** (power input): There is no data connection on this port, which is used only for the 5-volt power supply; power can be provided via the GPIO pins too, but that will bypass the protection fuse on the micro USB port, so use it with caution

- **System storage**: This is a **Micro SD** Card connector; you need to have one with a minimum of 4 GB, required for Raspbian OS using NOOBs

- **USB ports**: There are four USB 2.0 ports supporting up to 480 Mbps (only a single USB port on the A+ model)

Of course, like all computer systems where operation at the desktop level is programmed to be user friendly, once you peer beneath the surface of Pi at both the software and hardware level, it can get complicated.

To ensure that you have the best experience, please read through all of this chapter until you are ready to build and boot Raspbian for the first time and before you start to build your Pi development system.

After completing this chapter, you will be able to:

- Explain the features of the Raspberry Pi and its peripheral connections
- List the options for powering the Pi and the connected USB peripherals
- Summarize the SD Card software configuration options

- Build a bootable SD Card with a copy of the Raspbian OS
- Install Raspbian from the SD Card or the Internet
- Build and configure a working desktop system that boots directly to the graphical desktop interface

# Unboxing the Raspberry Pi

Although the Pi A+, B+, and Model 2-B are used for all of our projects, nothing covered in this book precludes the use of the older A and B models. The Pi you purchased might be sourced from many different suppliers. There are some critical differences that you need to be aware of if you plan to use the Pi for a hobby project or education tool:

| Model type | GPIO header | SD type | Audio / Composite video |
|---|---|---|---|
| Raspberry Pi A and Pi B | 26 pins | standard | Separate TRS and RCA connections |
| Raspberry Pi B+, A+ and Pi Model 2-B | 40 pins | micro | Combined into a single TTRS connector |

If you compare other revisions of the Pi with the following image, you will notice that there are some orientation and position changes for connectors and different mounting holes on the A+, B+, and Model 2-B as compared to the A and B models:

We suggest that you consider a complete kit of parts as a good starting point—if you haven't already bought your Pi. In particular, there are kits from Canakit.com for around $90. The kit includes everything needed for a new Pi project designer.

# Configure power for Pi

It is important to know that an insufficient power supply current capability could result in an installation that is unreliable and proves hard to diagnose when problems occur. It's OK to have a power supply capable of delivering more current than needed; the system only draws the current it requires.

The most common guidance for the Pi B is a 5-Volt power supply providing between 700 mA and 1 Amp and for the Pi B+ and Model 2-B, between 600 mA and 2 Amp. The higher power requirements for the Pi B+ and Pi 2-B (four USB connections) enable connection to a wide range of USB peripherals such as USB disks, portable printers, scanners, and so on.

Note that the Pi B+ and Pi 2-B have internal current limits of 600 mA set on the USB ports; exceeding the current will power off the port momentarily. The USB 2.0 specification recommends a maximum peripheral device current specification of 500 mA. You should ensure that heavy current peripherals are supported via an externally powered USB hub for the best reliability.

We used an **AmazonBasics** seven-port USB hub (see the following image) which has two ports that can provide over 1.2 Amp each, and five more ports that can provide up to 500 mA per port. It has a power supply rated for 5V at 4A, which cannot support maximum power on every port simultaneously (rarely required in any realistic configuration).

Our multi-Pi development environment is shown in the following image:

Before you can decide how to power your Pi, you must determine the highest level of current required to ensure that your devices can be properly supported in the configuration. We will continue to discuss power issues as they arise throughout the projects.

Our Pi is powered by a single AmazonBasics hub. The Pi and the hub are attached to a small piece of **medium-density fibreboard (MDF)** board using Velcro, which is an easy way to connect peripherals while designing a project. There is a WiFi adapter, keyboard, and mouse plugged into the hub. We normally connect via an Ethernet network interface, which facilitates the testing of a broader range of networking scenarios. You will notice in our configuration that a Pi-cam is connected and that we have a Microsoft webcam at the top of the right-hand side speaker.

A development desktop power/USB configuration like the one we showed in the preceding image will provide you with a stable development platform for our project designs. Of course, most final designs may require only the four USB ports on the motherboard and consume as little as 300 mA on average. The following list is the minimum configuration required to complete the projects in this book:

- A 5-V micro-USB power source rated at 2 A
- A USB mouse and keyboard

- An HDMI cable and an HDMI display, or an HDMI-to-DVI cable and a DVI display, or an HDMI-to-VGA convertor and a VGA LCD display
- An Ethernet cable and connection to your home network or a WiFi adapter for connecting to your WLAN

# Local display, keyboard, mouse, or remote headless access

To enable remote access to your Pi from a PC, Mac, or even a smartphone, you must first configure the bootloaders (the initial code that starts the processor) and the operating system on the SD card. Once you configure the OS, it's easy to make the Pi headless.

We use a physical monitor, keyboard, and mouse in our development environment. This configuration allows us to use the graphical desktop, see early error messages, and use advanced bootloader capabilities, such as multi-boot, to select from various configured operating systems that we build.

In our dual-Pi development environment, we have the screen, keyboard, and mouse connected to one Pi and then typically remote into the other using **PuTTy** or **MSTSC** (an RDP client) for remote access from a PC. Throughout this book, we will assume you have a connected keyboard, mouse, and display until a project actually requires a headless and wireless configuration.

# Selecting a screen

The most modern LCD monitors may have two or more HDMIs, or one HDMI and one DVI or **DisplayPort** — a much newer display standard). The Pi supports a single HDMI connection and a much more primitive composite video connection, neither of which can connect to VGA directly.

The Pi HDMI interface supports up to 1920 x 1200 pixels and provides the best possible desktop resolution. It may also support sound output over HDMI if the monitor includes speakers.

A composite video connection on the Pi can support up to 800 x 600 pixels depending on the monitor, most of which will typically only work at 640 x 480 pixels. However, a composite image could show some artifacts such as position errors or visible shading lines or bars. Composite monitors, which tend to be quite small, are often used for portable and auto-embedded systems.

When using the Pi, the following video output configurations are possible:

| Monitor type | Typical resolution | Required | Description |
|---|---|---|---|
| HDMI TV with built-in speakers | 1920 x 1080, 1280 x 720 | HDMI A – A cable | Dedicated or multi-source TV |
| HDMI monitor with or without speakers | 1920 x 1080, 1600 x 1024, 1280 x 800, 1440 x 900 | HDMI A – A cable | Dedicated or multi-source shared monitor |
| DVI monitor | 1920 x 1080, 1600 x 1024, 1280 x 800, 1440 x 900 | HDMI A – DVI – D cable | Dedicated or multi-source shared monitor |
| VGA monitor | 640 x 480, 720p, 1080i, 800 x 600, 1024 x 768 | HDMI-VGA convertor + VGA fifteen-pin Male – Male cable | Dedicated or multi-source shared monitor<br>Resolution is monitor dependant |
| Composite A/V | 640*480 | TRRS four-pin to RCA and audio | Small monitors |

The following image show the types of display/video cables that are supported with the Pi:

TRRS Audio and composite video          HDMI to HDMI          HDMI to DVI-D          Active HDMI to VGA

# Connecting VGA displays

We do not recommend the use of this type of display for a new user performing a NOOBS installation. To use a VGA screen for a NOOBS installation, you require configuration options that are beyond the scope of this book. If you complete your NOOBS installation with either a DVI or HDMI display (remember that most modern televisions have an HDMI connector), then it is a simple configuration task to enable the use of VGA displays via an HDMI-to-VGA convertor.

To enable output to a VGA display you need to make changes to the `config.txt` file in the `/boot` partition after the installation is complete. The following changes must be made to set VGA to 800 x 600:

```
hdmi_force_hotplug=1
hdmi_group=2
hdmi_mode=9
hdmi_drive=2
```

For VGA resolutions other than 800 x 600, visit `http://elinux.org/RPiconfig`.

If you have no other type of display available (composite, DVI, or HDMI) and must connect to a VGA display, while this is beyond the scope of this book, we recommend that you use **Berryboot** instead of NOOBS for the installation process. You can easily configure Berryboot for a headless install using VNC to provide remote access to the Berryboot menus. Please refer to the following websites for more information on Berryboot:

- `http://www.berryterminal.com/doku.php/berryboot`
- `http://www.berryterminal.com/doku.php/berryboot/headless_installation`

> The success of the HDMI-to-VGA convertors or cables can vary. The Raspberry Pi organization suggests that the **Pi-View** HDMI-to-VGA cable is always successful. For a datasheet on this device, go to `http://www.farnell.com/datasheets/1670850.pdf`.

# Getting your SD Card ready

Your Pi kit will typically include an SD Card. The Pi A and the Pi B use a standard-sized SD Card, and the Pi A+, B+, and Model 2-B use a Micro SD Card. Most of these SD Cards provided in kits are preconfigured with NOOBS. Once initialized, Raspbian or another optional operating system will install from an image already on the SD Card or from a network connection.

The minimum recommended SD Card size for the current version of Raspbian (February 2015 Debian 7:7.6 Wheezy) is 4 GB. This version results in a Raspbian install limited to a 2.7 GB partition. Most Pi kits come with a minimum SD Card size of 8 GB, allowing either multiple OS installations or a very large Raspbian partition.

The latest revision (1.4.0) of the new out-of-the-box software (NOOBS) is available in two versions:

- **NOOBS Version 1.4.0**: The vast majority of preconfigured SD Cards come with the full version of NOOBS (~700 MB), which includes an image of Raspbian on the card so you don't need an Internet connection to get started. Go to a download link later if you need to get latest the revisions or alternative OS's.

- **NOOBS lite Version 1.4.0**: This revision is small (only ~24 MB) but only supports getting your OS images from the network, so it could take longer to install depending on your network bandwidth. You will most likely always use this version when you buy a new SD Card and initialize it by yourself.

Depending on which version of Pi you have, you might need to have both the standard and Micro SD cards. We suggest that you only buy Micro SD cards that can be used for all Pi versions with a Micro SD-to-SD Card adapter.

With the addition of a Micro SD Card reader (Micro SD to USB), you have the greatest flexibility when formatting and initializing SD Cards. You can even reformat and initialize Micro SD Cards using the Pi once you have a working copy of Raspbian. The following image shows you the standard SD and the Micro SD Cards, and their capabilities:

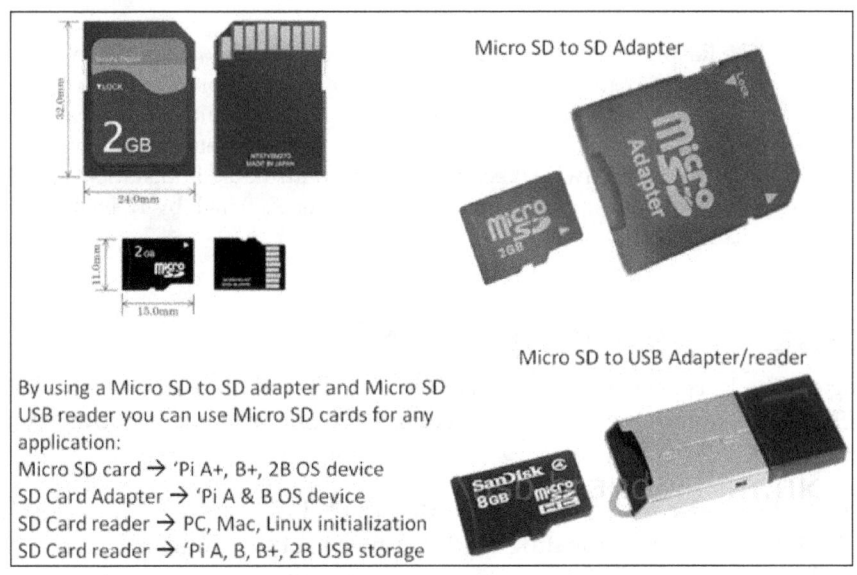

SD Cards have a specified speed or *Class*, typically Class 4 or Class 10. Class 4 cards are quite adequate for the application and typically cost less.

If you bought a kit with a prepared Micro SD Card, then you are ready to boot your Pi system. If you have a blank or previously used Micro or Standard sized SD Card, go to the Chapter 1 folder at http://1drv.ms/1ysAxkl to locate the *How to Initialize SD Card* instructions.

# Booting the Raspberry Pi for the first time

You are now ready to connect your Pi to a screen, keyboard, mouse, and a suitable power supply or USB hub. After inserting the Micro SD Card, you have one more decision to make—are you connecting to a network cable?

If you purchased an SD Card with a full copy of NOOBS or have just built the full copy (700 MB NOOBS install), then you don't need a network connection yet; you are ready to go.

If you built NOOBS Lite, you will need an Ethernet cable to connect to the network. Plug this cable into an Ethernet port on your network. The WAP or network needs to support DHCP, which is normally the way most home networks are configured. The IP address is allocated automatically when the Pi boots up and starts the NOOBS software.

> The Raspberry Pi does not come with a case, and you can potentially damage the card with static or by having connections short out on the motherboard. If the Pi is unprotected, you should ensure that all your cables are secured so that you reduce the potential to damage it in any way. Always keep your Pi on an insulated and static-free surface if it has no case. For example, we use a 9 inch by 12 inch piece of MDF board.

# It's time to power up the Pi

Powering up the Pi is easy, since there is no ON/OFF switch; you simply plug in the micro USB connection to the power connector. The following steps show you how to power up the Pi:

1. Plug it in and you can see that the **Red PWR LED** comes on and the **Green ACT LED** flashes, indicating read and write activity to the SD Card. These LEDs are near the GPIO header, as shown in the following image:

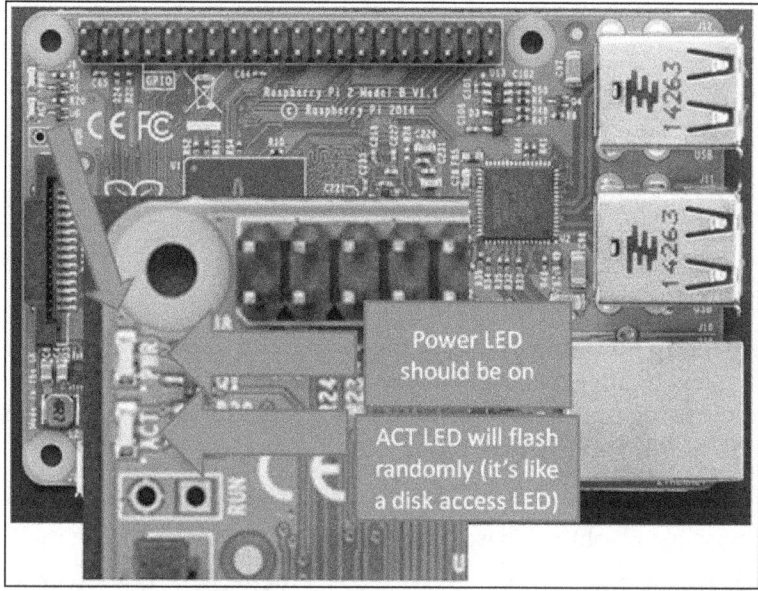

2. Next, you will see a brightly colored screen followed by some messages from NOOBS about resizing your partitions on the SD Card. Finally, there's a background with the Raspberry Pi logo, which is promptly covered by the NOOBS install window.

   The NOOBS install window shows the various OS options on the SD Card; you can select multiple options for the installation.

3. On the right-hand side of the install screen, there is an icon showing the options on the SD Card, and those that require network access. Selecting any of the options with a network icon will download from the Internet, provided you have a network connection.

4. Select the following options:

   ° **Raspbian**

   ° **Data Partition**

5. Click on **Install** to start the installation process.

6. A warning will ask you to confirm that you want the install to continue, click on **Yes**.

   At the bottom of the install window, it indicates the amount of space required to install these components (3275 MB or 3.2 GB). It will take about 25 minutes to install the software; a progress bar indicates what part of the process is currently being completed.

> Be careful not to accidentally power down your Pi during the installation process, as the partition table and the OS data are being rewritten, it is possible to corrupt the process and render the SD Card unusable. You won't damage the Pi or SD Card, but you might have to reinstall the NOOBS software to start again.

# No video on initial boot

When you power up your Pi, you will notice a flashing Green ACK LED followed by a video display. If, after the LED flashes, you don't see the display within a few seconds, try using one of the following key entries to resolve the issue; enter a numeric key to match your display type:

- Key 1: This sets the display to Standard HDMI mode. This mode will use the best possible resolution based on the EDID information from the display.

- Key 2: This sets the display to Safe HDMI mode. This is a low resolution 800 x 600 setting that can overcome displays with bad EDID information.

- Key 3: This sets the display to low resolution Composite PAL on the RCA connector for the Pi A and the Pi B and on the TRRS connector for the Pi A+, Pi B+, and Pi Model 2-B.

- Key 4: This sets the display to the low-resolution Composite NTSC on the RCA or TRRS connector.

If you discover that none of the key entries restores the display, check your cables or display functionality and then try the installation again.

# Final installation configuration

When the installation process is complete, you will be prompted to continue. Perform the following steps to configure your Pi:

1. Select **continue**; Pi will reboot and start Raspbian for the first time. You will now be presented with `raspi-config`; you can navigate the options using the arrow keys. This is a script that will modify configuration flags and files for options in the Raspbian OS.

2. Use the following settings to complete your configuration:
    - **Change User Password**: The default user is `pi` and the password is `raspberry`. For greater security, change from the default.
    - **Enable Boot to Desktop/Scratch**: Change this to Desktop Login as **pi** on the graphical desktop.

º **International options**: Change your time zone to suit your location and the keyboard layout to suit your keyboard. Typically, this will be set to the Generic 105 key (**Intl**) PC, English (**US**) or English (**GB**), **AltGR** to default, **Compose** to **No**, *Ctrl + Alt + Backspace* change to **Yes**.

º **Enable Camera**: Enable only if you have a Pi camera or intend to use one.

º **Add to Rastrack**: This is optional.

º **Overclock**: This is optional, but not suggested yet. If you do overclock, then ensure that the CPU has a heatsink attached to it.

º **Advanced Options**: **A2** is set for hostname (the default is **raspberrypi**); **A4** is set to enable an SSH server; **A6** is set to enable I2C; **A7** is set to disable kernel use of the serial port for messages and logon.

3. Select **Finish** and restart the computer to view the desktop, as shown in the following screenshot:

As the Raspberry Pi boots, you will see text roll up the screen; these are the boot messages as the OS dynamically builds the memory image. You will also see a Raspberry Pi logo in the top-left corner of the screen. One Raspberry indicates a single processor, and four Raspberries indicate the latest quad processor model 2-B.

# A quick tour of the desktop

After restarting your Pi, the Raspbian graphical desktop appears, and you are logged in as pi with the password as raspberry (if you did not change it).

Notice that the desktop is uncluttered. All the current GUI applications are located in the menu and five applications are on the quick launch bar. From the **Menu/Shutdown**, you can **Shutdown**, **Reboot**, or **Logout**. The following is a list of quick pointers of handy keyboard accelerators that you might find useful:

- *Ctrl* + *Alt* + *Backspace*: Use this key combination to log out of the current Xsession user (use Xsession to login).

- *Ctrl* + *Alt* + *F1*: Use this key combination to switch to a command session on tty1 (type exit to close)

- *Ctrl* + *Alt* + *F7*: Use this key combination to switch back to the graphical desktop

- *Ctrl* + *Alt* + *F2* through *F6*: Use this key combination to switch to a command session on tty2-tty6

# Instructions for downloading all project files

There are multiple downloadable files for each of the chapter projects, along with extra procedural documents; they are available for download from http://1drv.ms/1ysAxkl.

**Downloading the example code**

You can download the example code files for all Packt books you have purchased from your account at http://www.packtpub.com. If you purchased this book elsewhere, you can visit http://www.packtpub.com/support and register to have the files e-mailed directly to you.

You can access them from your Raspberry Pi desktop by performing the following steps:

1. Use the link `http://1drv.ms/1ysAxkl` in the web browser.

2. Use the OneDrive **Folder actions** dropdown.

3. Click on **Download folder** to download all the files to the default `/home/pi/Downloads` folder as a ZIP file.

4. Use **Xarchiver** to extract the files to the default destination folder `/home/pi/Downloads` and move them manually as required in each chapter project.

# Summary

Now that you've built and configured your Pi as a working desktop system that boots directly to the graphical desktop interface, let's review some of the important tasks you learned to perform:

- You built a hardware configuration for Raspberry Pi with locally connected peripherals

- You initialized and built a NOOBS SD card

- You booted NOOBS and then installed Raspbian locally or from the Internet

- You performed post install configuration selections with `raspi-config`

In the next chapter, you will use Raspbian desktop tools and the shell command line to build a talking clock using scripts and Python 3.

# 2
# Configuring the Raspberry Pi Desktop and Software

The Pi now boots to the desktop graphical interface, which means you have a base system on which to start project development. Like any other desktop PC, you will eventually want it configured to suit your development style. In this chapter, we maximize the utility of the desktop graphical tools and develop code for your projects. We don't expect you to become a Linux command-line guru. Instead, we will use simpler desktop tools such as editors, file managers, and the Python interactive development shell, **IDLE3**.

After completing this chapter, you will be able to:

- Install networking and graphical networking tools
- Keep your computer system up to date
- Configure the Pi desktop to suit your development needs
- Configure Ethernet and Wi-Fi networking connectivity options
- Explain code development options available by default
- Create Bash shell scripts and have them run automatically
- Create Python 3 scripts and have them installed to run automatically at boot

## Hardware and software networking configuration

Since we will need Internet connectivity to install tools and utilities, let's now look at the Pi hardware and software networking configuration in more detail; the wireless configuration is first since many project designers may prefer a wireless connection.

There are many Pi-compatible wireless adapters and you may even have bought one as part of your initial kit. The most common recommendation is that you use a Wi-Fi adapter that uses the **Realtek RTL8188CUS** chipset. The driver for this chipset (rtl8192cu) is included in the Raspbian distribution, so enabling this particular type of Wi-Fi adapter is easy.

First, you need to install the adapter, and then we will look at the connection status of the USB devices on the Pi to ensure it is detected:

1. Plug the Wi-Fi wireless adapter into any available USB port and unplug the Ethernet connection if you have one

2. Open a terminal window and type lsusb

3. In the same window, type lsusb -t

The lsusb results are printed as shown in the following screenshot:

Notice that lsusb gives a listing of the devices on the USB based on the bus (there is only one) and the device connection number. Refer to the preceding image; there are devices numbered from 1 to 9. The connection Bus: 1, Device: 8, is our Wi-Fi adapter (shown in the previous screenshot). You can see the mouse (DELL) and keyboard (DELL) in the listing.

The `lsusb -t` command gives a listing of the USB connection tree and some other interesting information. Sizing the USB tree is beyond the scope of this book; for now, you just need to know that the last number on the connection line shows the USB speed being used on that particular port. USB 2.0 high speed is shown as 480 Mbps; full speed is shown as 12 Mbps; and low speed is 1.5 Mbps.

You will often see these referred to as **USB 2.0**, **USB 1.1**, and **USB 1.0**. You can see from the listings that the wireless adapter is a Realtek RTL8188CUS802.11n WLAN adapter, the driver is `rtl8192cu`, and its USB connection speed is 480 Mbps.

Since we know that the Wi-Fi adapter is known to the system, you can configure the connection now. You will often see the Wi-Fi configuration utility referred to in configuration guides as the `wpa_supplicant` GUI user interface

The **wpa_gui** window shows **wlan0** as the adapter, but we don't yet have any networks to connect to. Let's add a network by completing the following steps:

1.  Unplug your Ethernet cable if it is plugged in.
2.  Open the **Wi-Fi Configuration** application by selecting **Menu | Preferences | Wi-Fi Configuration**.
3.  Click on the **Manage Networks** tab
4.  Click on **Scan**, which opens the **Scan results** window, and click on **Scan** again
5.  When the list of visible Wi-Fi networks appears in the **Scan results** window, double-click on your network, which will open the network properties window.
6.  In the network window, select the authentication type and enter your password or authentication keys
7.  Click **Add**
8.  Click **Close** on the **Scan results** window
9.  In the **wpa_gui** window, your network should be populated in the **Manage Networks** tab. Click on the **Current Status** tab and then click on **Connect**. The connection to your WAP should occur within just a few seconds, but it may take several more seconds until an IP address is finally allocated.
10. Test your connectivity using the web browser to access the Internet. When you close the **wpa_gui** window, it will minimize to an icon on the right-hand side of your taskbar. From there, you can open it again, monitor or alter your wireless connection, or close the application entirely.

11. The following screenshot shows you the various windows you come across when connecting to WiFi:

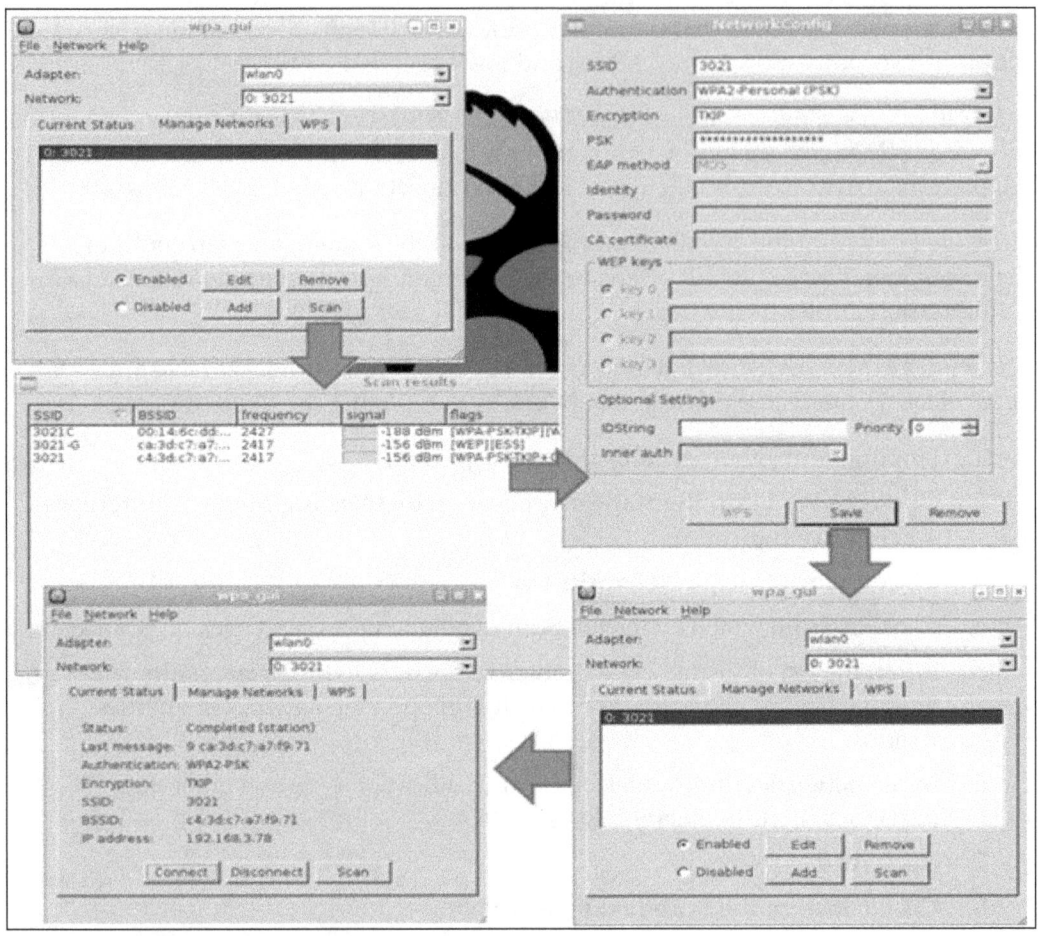

In most cases, setting up Ethernet is a simple task. You just plug in the cable. This is because, by default, the Pi Ethernet connection is set to DHCP, and the IP address settings are provided over the Ethernet network from your router. By default, there is no nice GUI screen to set up Ethernet. You would need to specify a static IP address and mask from the command line.

There is an easier way to complete this task. Perform the following steps to install a utility called **Wicd Network Manager**:

1. Open a **Terminal** session and type `sudo apt-get -y install wicd-gtk`.

2. When the package has been installed, you can start it from **Menu | Internet | Wicd Network Manager**. The installation also sets the **WiCD** daemon to start each time you boot the computer.

3. The **Wicd Network Manager** windows should show all the available wireless networks (you are still connected to your wireless network), and you can set up all the required configuration details in this interface.

4. Plug in your Ethernet cable (connected to your home network) and click on **Refresh**.

   In the **Wicd Network Manager** window, you will see that both Ethernet and wireless network configurations can be managed. You won't see the wired Ethernet management interface options unless you are connected to an Ethernet network.

5. Click on the **Properties** button of your **Wired Network** connection to get the **Wired Network – Properties** page for your Ethernet connection. From here, you can configure static IP and DNS settings. The following screenshot shows how you can accomplish this:

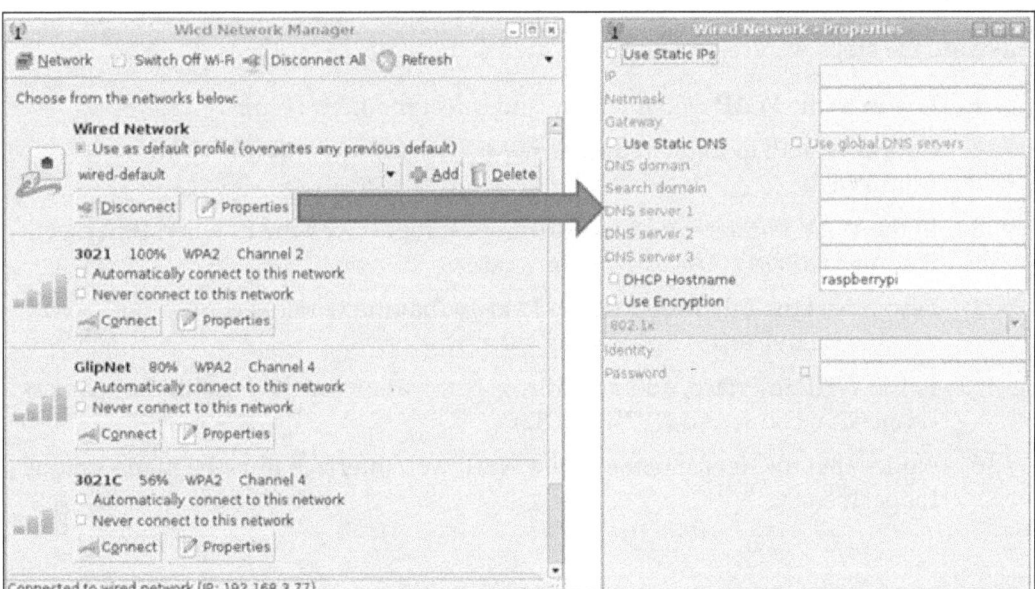

You can manage the properties of both the wired and wireless configurations from Wicd or leave the wireless connection managed by **wpa_gui**. Both utilities will add an icon on the right-hand side of the taskbar when you run them (if you are connected to Wi-Fi). The Wicd utility will shut down if there is no wlan connection, but the **wpa_gui** utility will remain in the taskbar.

# Client reservations for Ethernet and wireless

By default, IP addresses are allocated to a device using the DHCP protocol for most home **Wireless Access Points** (**WAPs**) and routers. While clients usually get the same IP address issued each time they start, it is possible under some circumstances that a new address could be allocated. Most professional IT people would suggest that, if you want to be sure that the same IP address is issued at all times, you should configure the client (in this case the Pi) to use a static IP address.

There is a much simpler way to achieve the same end result, which is to have an effectively static IP address for the client. In most WAPs, you can set a client IP address reservation. This tells the WAP (on both wireless and wired connections) to always issue the same IP address while still using DHCP for a particular device's MAC address (the base identifier of the wireless adapter or the Ethernet adapter).

While the interface to your WAP might be different from ours (**WNDR3700**), how you configure it is very similar.

Here are the steps we used to configure the WAP:

1. Log in to the **WAP** web interface and select the **LAN** setup.
2. Connect the Pi to the wired Ethernet network and verify the IP address from **Wicd.**
3. In the WAP interface, add an address reservation for the Pi when Ethernet is connected (192.168.3.77 in my case).
4. Disconnect the Ethernet cable and verify that the wireless connection becomes active again upon using **Wicd.**
5. In the WAP interface, add an address reservation for the Pi with the wireless connection connected (192.168.3.82).
6. Notice that the device name in the WAP web interface must be made unique for each entry.

You can follow a similar procedure even if you don't have the same brand of WAP (menus might be somewhat different). Then, whenever you connect to the network using either Ethernet or wireless, you will always be issued with the same IP address.

# Configuring the Raspberry Pi desktop and software

Because you enabled boot to the graphical desktop during the final installation configuration in *Chapter 1, Getting Started with Raspberry Pi*, each time you boot the Pi, the desktop automatically appears. The Pi is now very much like a compact version of your desktop PC, laptop, or even iPad.

The desktop environment is called the **lightweight X11** desktop environment (**LXDE**). It is installed on top of a window manager, which in this case is **Openbox**. Let's take a quick tour of some important elements of the desktop, and at the same time set up some preferences and options.

The information to follow will provide you with the guidance you need to install a screensaver package and set up a desktop accelerator:

- On the left-hand end of the taskbar is the main menu icon. When you click on it, one menu option offered is the ability to shut down. If you click on the shutdown menu selection, the **End Session** window opens. This allows you to select **Logout**, **Reboot** your Pi, or **Shutdown**.

- Try clicking on the selection to shut down and notice the ACT LED on the Pi motherboard as the computer shuts down.

- When you start the shutdown process, the video display will clear very quickly, but your system is not yet shut down. Notice that the ACT LED flashes for many more seconds, which is the OS writing changes to the file system on the SD Card. The following screenshot illustrates the start of the shutdown process:

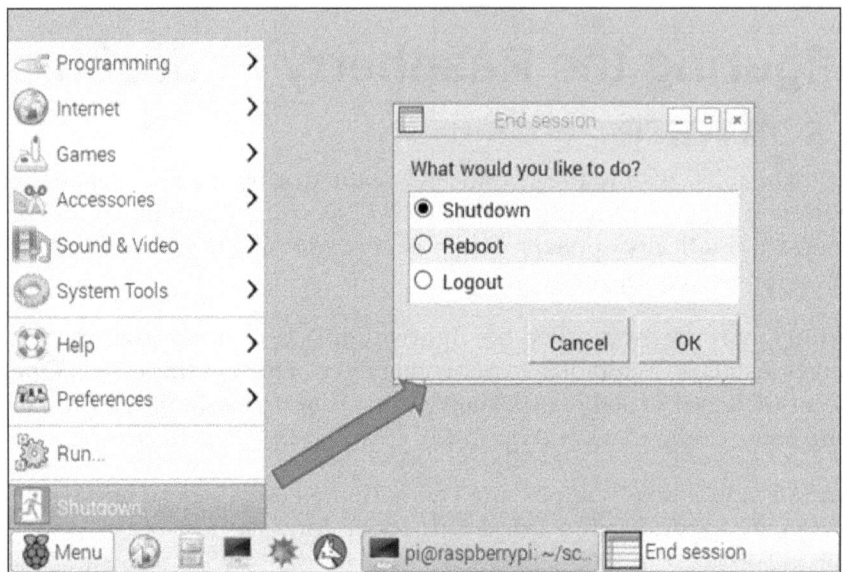

You will probably need to wait for at least 20 seconds (about 10 seconds for the Pi Model 2-B) before it is safe to pull out the power connector. There is no absolute way to ensure the shutdown is complete, so make sure that you wait for a few seconds after you see the last activity. The last activity is ten regular flashes of the ACT LED.

If you pull the power out while the system is running during the shutdown process or while updates to the SD Card are being made, it can corrupt the filesystem. After mostly random flashes, the last activity results in about 10 regular LED flashes as the OS updates the drive.

# Keeping the development environment up to date

Now that your Pi development desktop environment is configured, there is one remaining task to complete. You need to manage updates as you add or change the installed packages. This task includes any updates made to the OS and packages for version changes, security, and bug fixes.

There is no automated notification of updates or bug fixes to keep software up to date. You can routinely schedule the following three command-line commands:

| Command | Description |
|---|---|
| `sudo apt-get update` | This command flags updates required for all your installed components and packages |
| `sudo apt-get upgrade` | This command will upgrade your OS and applications if there has been a revision, but it never deletes files (so it is possible, and challenging, to back the changes out) |
| `sudo apt-get autoremove` | This command helps to remove packages and files where they were loaded as a dependency and are no longer needed |

If you build a Pi project and the system is stable and running, then it may be less important to perform updates or upgrades.

 If you install new packages, it is worth your time to ensure that the system is up to date using the aforementioned commands. In addition, if your project is directly exposed to the Internet, consistent upgrades will ensure good security.

# Setting up a screensaver

There is no screensaver in the default Raspbian installation. However, we can enable one by installing the X11 screensaver package. Once this package is installed, you can configure a screensaver and even lock your desktop for security. Let's do that installation now:

1. Open a **Terminal** session (click the terminal icon in the quick-launch tray), which will take you to a Terminal session command line.
2. Type `sudo apt-get -y install xscreensaver` to install the X11 screensaver package on your system using root privileges.
3. Wait for the package to install.
4. Click on **Menu | Preferences | Screensaver**.
5. In the **Screensaver Preferences** window, set the mode to **Only One Screen Saver**.

6.  Select **XLYap** as the screensaver.

7.  Set **Blank After** to **1 minute**.

8.  Enable **Lock Screen After** and set the time value to **0 minutes**. This causes the screensaver to lock the screen as soon as it activates.

9.  Close the window to save your changes.

The following screenshot encapsulates the actions performed in the preceding list of steps:

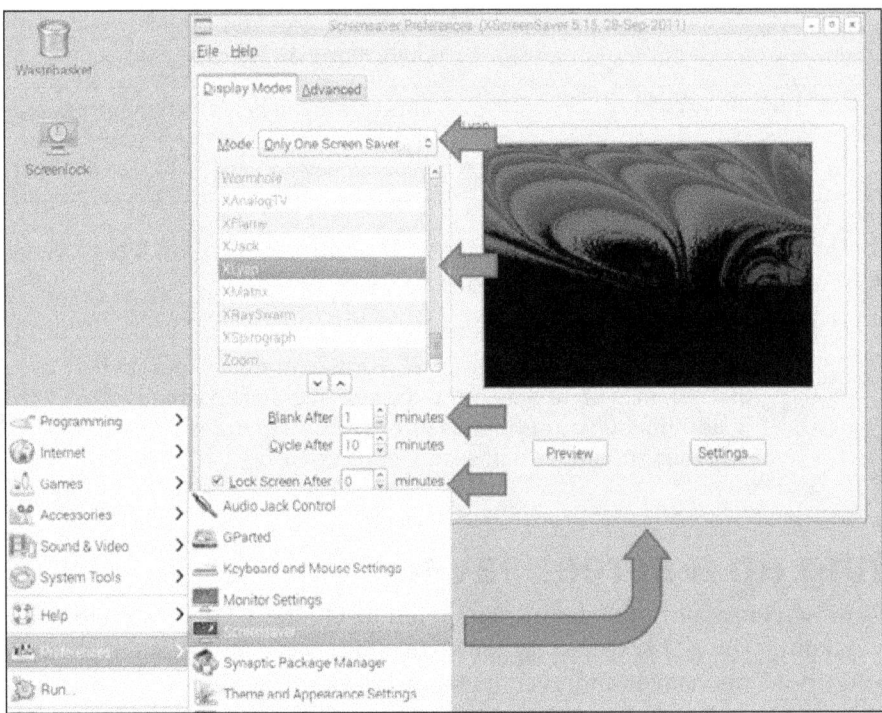

Don't touch the mouse or keyboard for 1 minute, then the screensaver will activate. When you move the mouse or hit a key to go back to the desktop, then a login screen will appear. Once you enter the username (pi) and the password (raspberry, by default), your desktop will appear again.

Set your screensaver preference (I prefer just a blank screen) and the **Blank After** interval to some acceptable number of minutes. If you don't want the screen to go blank or go to a screensaver at all, then select **Disable Screensaver** in the **Screensaver Preferences** window. Disabling the screensaver is very useful for projects where you have no mouse or keyboard and you want the screen always visible.

We have now configured a screensaver that will activate after a fixed delay, but it's also nice to be able to manually activate the screensaver.

# Manually locking your session

Next, you will set up a desktop application shortcut that immediately locks your session. You are going to create a special file type that the system understands as containing information to run a particular program within the graphical environment. In many cases, the files are of the form `xyz.desktop` although the file extension does not actually need to exist. The following steps show you how to create a desktop screen lock:

1. Click on **Menu | Run** to start the **Run** form prompt window.

2. Type `lxshortcut -o /home/pi/Desktop/Screenlock`, and hit *Enter* or click on **OK**.

3. An **Application Shortcut** form will appear; fill in the following details:

   1. In the **Name** field, type in `Screenlock`

   2. In the **Command** field, type `xscreensaver-command -lock`

   3. In the **Tooltip** field, type `Lock the Screen`

   4. Click on **Change Icon** and highlight the **kscreensaver** icon. Click on **OK** to select the icon.

   5. Click on **OK** in the **Application Shortcut** form.

4. The **Screenlock** icon will appear on your desktop.

5. Right-click on the **Screenlock** icon and open with the **Leafpad** editor.

6. The text in the **Screenlock** desktop shortcut file provides all the information required to send a command to `xscreensaver` to lock and should be as follows:

```
[Desktop Entry]
Encoding=UTF-8
Type=Application
Name=Screenlock
Name[en_GB]=Screenlock
Icon=kscreensaver
Exec=xscreensaver-command -lock
Comment[en_GB]=Lock the Screen
StartupNotify=true
```

7. Close the text editing window.

8. Double-click on the **Screenlock** icon and your screensaver will immediately activate.

Be aware that, if you use screensavers that require a lot of CPU resources, then your applications might run slowly when the screensaver is active. On the single processor Pi's, CPU resources used may approach 80-90 percent for a computationally intense single-threaded screensaver. While on the quad processor Pi, although one processor may have high utilization, the overall quad processor utilization will generally be less than 25 percent.

# Desktop and file manager accelerators

When you work in a graphical desktop, one of the most used utilities is the file manager (**PCManFM**). In a development environment, there is often the need to transition from a low-security-privilege (user) context to a high-security-privilege (root) context to complete tasks. The current file manager does not allow this to happen. PCManFM will allow you to add defined actions to its context menus that can help to reduce the need for low-level command-line editors and Terminal session commands. In addition, there could be a constant need to start multiple **Terminal** windows and to move between multiple desktop views to reduce the clutter of open windows.

Now, let's set up a useful desktop accelerator. Find a clear location on the desktop with your mouse pointer and right-click on it. The menu that comes up is from the file manager and is not usually very useful. To replace it with some new functionality, follow these steps:

1. Right-click on the desktop and select **Desktop Preferences**.

2. In the **Desktop Preferences** window, select the **Advanced** tab.

3. Select **Show menus... from the window manager** and close the window.

4. Find a clear spot on your desktop and, when you right-click now, a new menu will appear with accelerators to start a **Terminal** window and the default web browser or switch between desktop windows. I hope you find this desktop accelerator much more useful.

5. To clear this option and return to the original settings, launch a Terminal window and type `pcmanfm --desktop-pref`:

    ° Note that there are two instances of "-" before `desktop-pref`

    ° On **Advanced tab**, deselect the **Show menus provided by window manager...** option

The following screenshot captures the actions performed in the preceding list of steps:

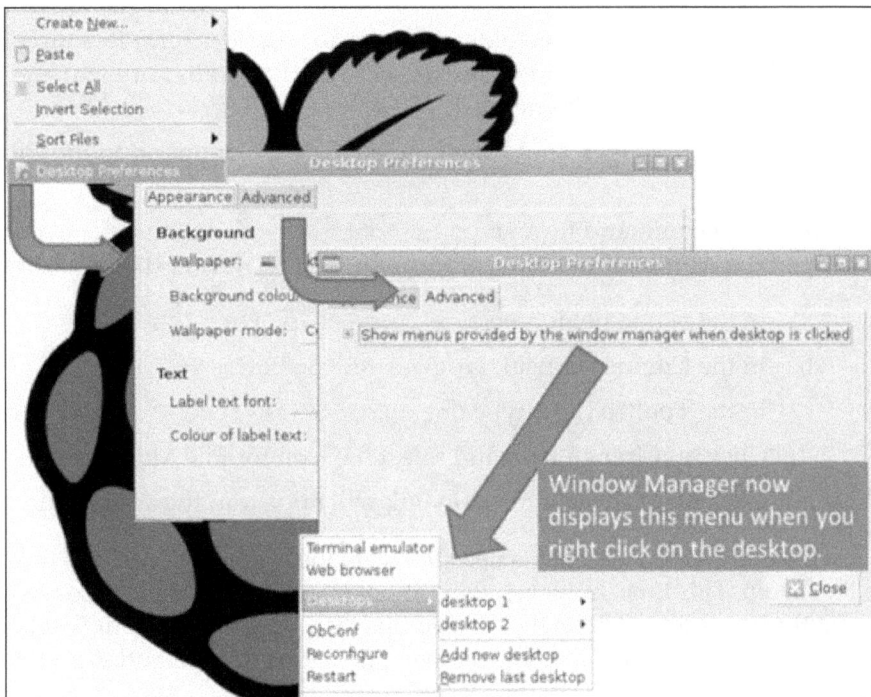

Now you will learn how to add root privileges to the PCManFM file manager.

# Adding root privileges to the PCManFM file manager

The following steps show you how to add the root privileges to the PCManFM file manager:

1. Open **File Manager** from the application launch bar. By default, it will open focused on the /home/pi location.

2. Click on **View** and select **Show Hidden**, which will show hidden files (those that start with a period).

3. Set the **File Manager** focus to the /home/pi/.local/share folder.

4. Right-click on the right-hand side pane in **File Manager**, select **Create New/Folder**, and name the folder file-manager.

5. Double-click on the file manager directory and then create a subfolder called `actions`.

6. Double-click on the **actions** folder, and the address **Uniform Resource Identifier** (**URI**) should show `/home/pi/.local/share/file-manager/actions`; the directory is empty.

7. From the **File Manager Tools** menu, select **Run a Command in the Current Folder.**

8. In the **Run a command** form, type `lxshortcut -o ./OpenAsRoot.desktop` to open the **Application Shortcut** form. In the form, enter the following:

   a. In the **Name** field, type `Open folder as root`

   b. In the **Command** field, type `gksudo pcmanfm %u`

   c. In the **Tooltip** field, type `Open folder as root`

   d. Click on **Change Icon** and select the icon for File Manager

   e. Click on OK, and a desktop link will appear in the **actions** directory

You've just used the same method we used to create the Screenlock desktop link to create a link again. This time, however, the content is not quite complete, so we will have to edit the file. Right-click on the file and open it with the text editor (Leafpad). Change the text in the file to match the following desktop entry definition and then close and save the file:

```
[Desktop Entry]
Encoding=UTF-8
Type=Action
Name=Open Folder as Root
Name[en_GB]=Open Folder as Root
Comment[en_GB]=Open Folder as Root
Profiles=on-directory;
Icon=file-manager
StartupNotify=true

[X-Action-Profile on-directory]
MimeTypes=inode/directory;
SelectionCount=1
Exec=gksudo pcmanfm %u
Name=Open as Root
```

After you save the file, you can click on **Menu | Shutdown | Logout** and then log in as the user `pi` with your password. This reloads the file manager and will add the action to the menus.

 Log in using the default Xsession; don't use the LXDE or Openbox sessions.

You can open **File Manager** from the Application Launch bar and right-click on any directory to get the **File Manager** context menu, as shown in the image below. Note that the second-to-last entry is **Open Folder as Root**. This is the menu item we have just added.

Click on **Open Folder as Root** and a new **File Manager** window will open. This window opens with root privileges and has an exclamation mark (!) in an orange triangle that indicates a **superuser** privilege. Any tools used within the new window, such as Leafpad editing sessions or Terminal sessions, will have a root-privileged user. And any files you create will have root ownership.

One minor annoyance with our new root-privileged **File Manager** is that the home directory is set to /root instead of /home/pi. To correct this, you can open **Edit | Preferences** in the **File Manager** window, and in the **Preferences | Advanced** tab, set the home folder to **Custom** and enter /home/pi as the location. This setting is remembered by File Manager.

 Using root privilege provides you with the permission to do almost anything (good or bad consequences), and you should only raise your privilege level when you absolutely have to complete a function or task at that level.

Once you have created the additional action menu item, the File Manager folder context menu will be as shown in the following image. In the context menu, the original item called **File Manager** opens a new tab within the same instance of **File Manager**. The new item, **Open Folder as Root**, will launch a new instance of **File Manager** with root privileges. The following screenshot shows the additional entry in the PCManFM directory context:

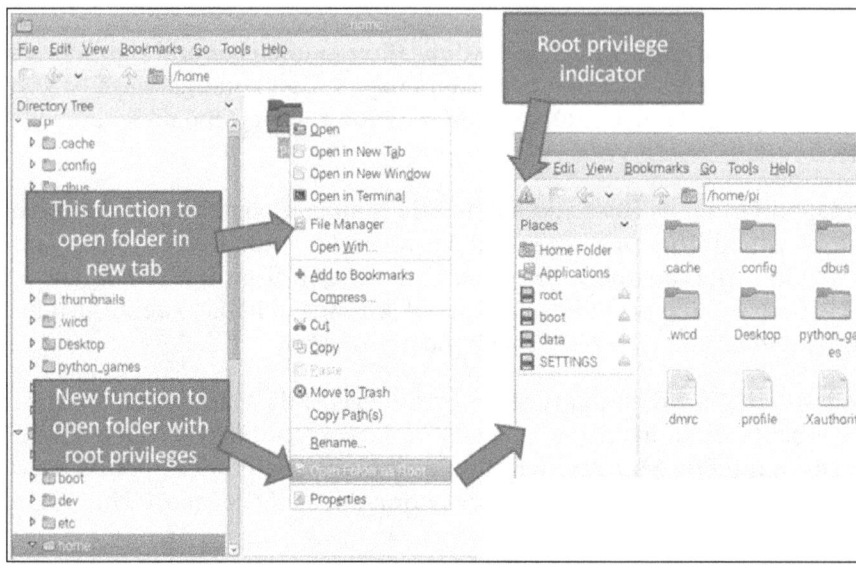

# Programming on the Raspberry Pi

Now let's look at the Pi as a development tool; we need to understand the options available in Pi. There are a plethora of languages and scripts that might be used to program project functionality. Here are some options for development immediately available in your Raspbian release:

| Programming language | Skill level | Built-in | URL |
| --- | --- | --- | --- |
| Bash | Simple to advanced | Yes | https://www.packtpub.com/networking-and-servers/linux-shell-scripting-cookbook-second-edition |
| C | Medium to advanced | Yes | http://www.linuxtopia.org/online_books/programming_books/gnu_c_programming_tutorial/index.html |
| Python 2, 3 | Simple to advanced | Yes | https://www.packtpub.com/hardware-and-creative/raspberry-pi-cookbook-python-programmers |

# Developing with Bash shell scripts

**Bash** is the shell used to start the **Terminal** command-line interface. Bash shell scripts are groups of commands that act much like a simple programming language, but they are limited to the functions exposed in Bash. Bash scripts are typically used to automate administration tasks in Linux-based systems. Because they can be used to invoke executables, they can also be used to provide flexibility in non-administrative tasks.

While you may never use complex Bash scripts to manage your Pi, scripts can provide you with quite a simple way to achieve automated functionality in a project.

# Project 1 – Building a talking clock with a Bash script

This project will expose you to the Bash shell scripting language. You will build a talking clock that tells the time every minute using an executable and an Internet-based web service. Once the clock is up and running, you will use an automation tool called **Cron** to schedule and run tasks at a particular time or at regular intervals.

The talking clock will have the following features and functions:

- Automatically start every minute and run in the background without any visible interface to the desktop user
- Read the system time to get the local time on your Pi
- Produce a correctly formatted time string to announce the time, for example, you might say "*The time is now nine fifteen AM*"
- Convert the time string to audio and play it
- Exit the script

# Creating project files and directories

First, you will open a **Terminal** window to create the project files and directories, update our system, and load a new utility application:

1.  At the command line of the terminal session, complete the following steps:

| Command | Description |
| --- | --- |
| Type `mkdir   ./tclock` and hit *Enter* | This creates the project directory |
| Type `mkdir ./tclock/bin` and hit *Enter* | This creates a directory where the executable files are kept |
| Type `touch ./tclock/bin/tclock.sh` and hit *Enter* | This creates an empty file that we use to hold our script |
| Type `chmod +x ./tclock/bin/tclock.sh` and hit *Enter* | This marks the script file properties as executable |

Now, you need a new utility package called **mpg123** to play the audio.

2.  At the command line of the terminal session type:

| Command | Description |
| --- | --- |
| Type `sudo  -s` and hit *Enter* | This turns on the root privileges |
| Type `apt-get  update` and hit *Enter* | This flags all package updates for the installed system |
| Type `apt-get  upgrade` and hit *Enter* | This updates the binaries and files |
| Type `apt-get -y install mpg123` and hit *Enter* | This installs the application to play a `.mpg` file to the headphones |
| Type `exit` and hit *Enter* | This turns off the root privileges |

 Since the audio has not been configured, the default sound output will be presented on the combined audio/video connector. You can plug any 3.5 mm stereo headphone or powered computer speakers into this connector, but it will prevent the use of composite video unless you have a breakout Y cable. If you are connected to an HDMI display with speakers (like a television) your default sound may be over HDMI. Do not plug in alternative audio adapters at this time, as new audio defaults must be configured.

Using the mpg123 audio utility, you can now test how to produce an audio stream for the talking clock. You could create files for each of the words we need to produce, concatenate them together, and then play the file. However, there is a much quicker and less onerous way to do this. Google has a web-based text-to-speech browser-based service and, since our Pi is connected to the Internet either by Ethernet or Wi-Fi, we can take advantage of this service.

To test out the web service, open an instance of the web browser from the taskbar. In the address bar, type:

```
http://translate.google.com/translate_tts?tl=en&q=The time is 9 15 am
```

The web page rendered has an audio player on it and will announce the time through your headphones or speakers. Notice that it does take a couple of seconds for the translation to occur and for the speech stream to return. Since we only require a one-minute resolution, we think that you will find this delay acceptable.

Now that you know the format of the string (limited to 100 characters maximum), you will need to submit it to the Google **text-to-speech** (**tts**) web service to get the audio stream returned. In order to avoid errors in translation, it is important that you use this format consistently when submitting the request to the tts service.

To produce the string data, use the Bash script file you created earlier. You will edit the script in Leafpad using the following steps:

1. Open **File Manager** and browse to /home/pi/tclock/bin.

2. Right-click on tclock.sh and select **Leafpad Text Editor**.

3. Type the following lines of text into tclock/bin/tclock.sh:

```
#! /bin/bash
#called a shebang this provides the correct executable path

HR=$(date +%l)      #variable holds the 12 hour time value
MIN=$(date +%M)     #variable holds the minutes time value
MD=$(date +%p)      #variable holds the AM/PM indicator for the 12
hour clock
String="The time is $HR   $MIN   $MD"
#Execute mpg123 with a url that will return am mpg stream to be
played
#The -q flag suppresses any text output
mpg123  -q  'http://translate.google.com/translate_
tts?tl=en&q='"$String"
```

4. Close the file and save the changes on exit.

5. In **File Manager**, click on **F4** (open the current folder in a Terminal session).

6. At the command line of the terminal session, type `./tclock.sh`

Each time you start the `./tclock.sh` command, you should hear the time string in the headphones or speakers (click on the up arrow in the Terminal session window to step through the command history and repeat the command). You should hear that the sound produced in the stereo headphones has some background noise. While this might be OK for simple audio functionality such as this project, it is not suitable for any serious music appreciation. You can improve the sound quality output by adding new hardware as discussed in a later chapter on audio input and output.

In the next task, we will configure the script to run automatically every minute and, to do this, we will add the script to a list of cron tasks. A cron is a job scheduler that uses a defined table (`crontab`) to specify what to run and when.

You need a new utility package called **gnome-schedule** to provide the desktop application to edit cron jobs. To install the cron GUI, type the following commands at the Terminal session command line:

| Command | Description |
|---|---|
| `sudo -s` | This turns on root privileges |
| `apt-get update` | This gets the latest updates |
| `apt-get upgrade` | This upgrades any files that are required |
| `apt-get install gnome-schedule` | This utility allows the editing of cron jobs |
| `exit` | This turns off root privileges |

Once gnome-schedule is installed, you will have a new application under **Menu | System Tools | Scheduled tasks** (log out and log in again to refresh the Menu). To add our clock script in the **Scheduled Tasks** application, complete the following steps:

1. In the Configure scheduled-tasks window, select **New**.

2. **In the Add a Scheduled Task form, select A Task that launches recurrently**.

3. In the **Create a New Scheduled Task** form, fill out the name of the task and the file path (`/home/pi/tclock/bin/tclock.sh`) to the script file and then select **Advanced**.

4. Select **Edit** on the **Minutes** line.

5. In the **Edit minute** form select **Every minute**.

6. Click on **OK** and the then on **Apply**.

7. Accept the warning on the home directory for tasks.

8. Your task is now shown in the **Configure Scheduled Tasks** window.

9. Close the **Configure Scheduled Tasks** window.

The following screenshot illustrates the steps mentioned in the preceding list:

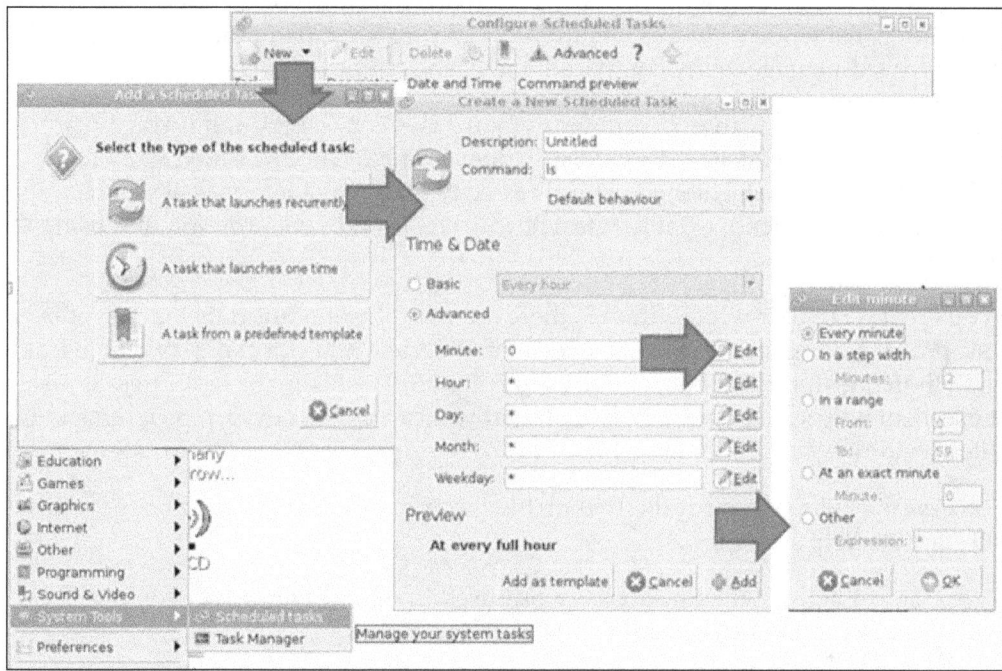

Cron uses the system time to run jobs. Now that it is synced with the rollover of the minutes on the system clock, you should hear the time announced on the headphones or speakers. Although this was a relatively easy project, you can now create a simple script. Also, you've experienced some of the power available when using Bash.

After examining the **man** pages for bash, date, and mpg123, you might want to make a few changes to the functionality of the talking clock. Here are some updates that we think you might find worth considering:

1. Add day and date announcements to the time (remember the 100-character limit).

2. Change the clock to a 24-hour count.

3. Have the time in different time zones announced.

4. Write the .mpg audio file output to disk to build a word vocabulary for offline use of the clock.

We will revisit the *Talking Clock* script again when we add button functionality (*Chapter 5*, *Port Input and Output on the Raspberry Pi*).

# Building a talking clock with Python 3

Python is often used as a scripting language when the speed of execution is a secondary consideration. In this situation, it can provide much more script flexibility and improved manageability compared to a Bash script.

The GUI development environment for Python 3 is called IDLE3, and if you double-click on the icon, it will, by default, open a single window called Python Shell. Although you can enter commands directly in the shell interface, it will be beneficial for you to learn from the start how to create and save program files using the Python editor.

If you are not familiar with Python 3, there are many online tutorials that introduce basic programming techniques. An excellent overview and tutorial is available from the Python.org website at `http://docs.python.org/3.2/tutorial`. There is also an excellent help system in Python Shell that you can use to develop programs in the editor window.

To access the help system, at the Python Shell command prompt, type `help()`; this will start the help system:

- To get help on the **import** keyword used in our talking clock program, type `import` at the help prompt
- The import keyword causes a module to be loaded, and you can type `modules` to see all of them listed
- The module we load first in the program is the **time** module; get help on that by typing `time` at the help prompt

When developing a program in IDLE3, if you leave Python Shell at the help prompt and start the program in the editor window, it will generate another instance of Python Shell.

To continue building the talking clock in Python 3, go to the `Chapter 2 Supplemental Materials` folder at `http://1drv.ms/1ysAxkl` to locate the `Project 1a: Building a Talking Clock with Python 3` document.

This additional content will show you how to implement the talking clock using Python to call the Bash script and then how to use only Python. The Python implementations do not need to use cron to schedule the task; it can be loaded every time the computer starts up and run independent of the scheduler.

# Summary

Now that we've completed the second chapter, let's review some of the important tasks you performed in this chapter:

- Installed graphical networking tools
- Configured the Pi desktop to suit your development needs
- Configured the Ethernet and Wi-Fi networking connectivity options
- Created a talking clock to better understand Bash scripts and Python 3 programming language

You also learned how to do most of this work directly from the desktop, minimizing the use of command-line sessions.

At some point in your project design career, you may want to become a command-line geek, but it would require building expertise at the command-structure level.

In the next chapter, you will learn how to connect PiCam or multiple webcams and to acquire and store video streams and images.

# Raspberry Pi and Cameras

3

Most laptops and tablets now come with multiple high-resolution video cameras. Also, most desktops eventually include a camera for video conferencing and video messaging. We expect that camera technology will provide high resolution, good color rendering, and smooth camera image acquisition in our applications. However, achieving this capability requires a great deal of processor power and very advanced hardware interfaces.

After completing this chapter, you will be able to:

- Configure the Raspberry Pi to support both webcam and PiCam video solutions
- Install graphical tools to configure partitions to manage file space for video storage
- Install applications and utilities to test cameras and sense motion with cameras
- Create Bash shell scripts for video acquisition
- Create Python 3.0 scripts for video acquisition

## Connecting cameras to the Raspberry Pi

Let's consider how cameras connect to the Pi. Hardware simplification has resulted in a low-cost product with the majority of the hardware interfaces built into a single **System on Chip (SOC)**.

Here is a summary of two types of cameras that can be easily connected to the Pi motherboard:

- **MIPI Camera Serial Interface (CSI)** camera: This interface is built into the SOC and significantly reduces CPU load when acquiring video by automatically moving complete frames from the camera into the CPU/GPU memory.

- **USB connected webcams**: This interface (USB) is built into the SOC but is not capable of the same level of performance that you would find in laptops, tablets, or desktop machines. The CPU is much more involved in moving video line and frame data and, therefore, more CPU resources are consumed. Since there are multiple USB ports on the Pi, it can support multiple cameras, but each consumes more CPU resources.

To gain a better understanding of the relative performance of the two camera connection types, review the following table:

| Camera | 320 x 240 fps | CPU percent | 640x480 fps | CPU percent |
|---|---|---|---|---|
| PiCam/Pi NoIR (CSI) | 25-90 | <2 (3-5) | 25-90 | <2 (3-5) |
| Microsoft LifeCam Studio (USB) | 30 (13) | 60 (35) | 11 (5) | 40 (45) |
| eMPIA Microscope Camera (USB) | 8.1 (4.1) | 16 (25) | 8.1 (4.1) | 20 (25) |
| Logitech QuickCam Pro 6000 (USB) | 30 (14) | 75 (33) | 12 (6) | 49 (45) |

Note that the parameters in parentheses in the preceding table are for the single-processor Raspberry Pi (A, B, A+, and B+), while the others are for the quad processor Raspberry Pi 2 Model B at default clock speeds. The CPU percentage for the quad processor is the average over all four processors.

# PiCam and PiNoIR

The Raspberry Pi PiCam or PiNoIR (the same camera with no infrared filter) connects to the MIPI Camera Serial Interface. While there is only a single connector on the Pi B+ motherboard, a future update could include multiple cameras with a plug-on daughterboard.

There are some limitations with the PiCam. The restricted length of the interface cable means that you need to mount the camera and Pi close together. This restriction tends to limit the size and flexibility of the camera head. We rate the performance of the PiCam very highly. If you need to capture high-resolution and/or high-frame-rate videos, there is currently no better solution for the Pi. The PiCam can acquire video data at full HD 1080 pixel video @ 30 FPS, 720 pixel video @ 60 FPS, and static images up to 2592 x 1944. If you need further information on this camera, simply search the web for PiCam or visit

```
http://www.raspberrypi.org/help/camera-module-setup/.
```

# Webcams

As stated in the introduction, most webcams provide high-performance and high-resolution USB-based video. For a new desktop or mobile device, they can be purchased at relatively low prices. However, they cannot provide the same level of video performance when connected to the Pi.

When webcams are connected to a Pi, they must share the USB channel with other high-data-rate peripherals such as the Ethernet controller or a Wi-Fi adapter. Image acquisition places a higher demand on CPU resources as compared to laptops, tablets, and desktops. Still, most webcams are equipped with a long-connection cable (for example, Microsoft LifeCam has a 10-foot cable), which can be beneficial for camera placement.

# Project architecture for the Raspberry Pi security camera

To learn more about connecting cameras to the Pi, let's start a project that builds a motion-sensitive security system using multiple cameras.

For this project, our security system will perform the following activities:

- It will run for a day on an 8 GB SD card Raspbian install, but it should never be allowed to use up all the storage space

- It will start automatically after a power failure and when the system reboots.

- It will support at least two cameras, of which one may be the PiCam or PiNoIR.

- It will use a webcam image resolution of either 320 x 240 or 640 x 480 to provide movement detection.

- It will maintain high-quality PiCam image resolution while keeping the video file storage at an acceptable level.

The following diagram shows the proposed project architecture:

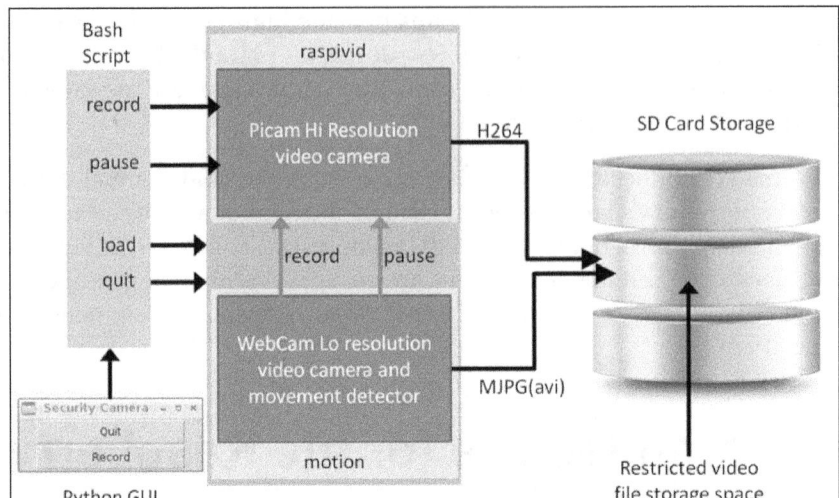

We will continue to explain the features of the preceding architecture as we progress through this chapter.

# Features and limitations of the cameras

Since we still need to understand the limits of each of the cameras, we will start by acquiring some camera data. If you have only one camera connected, that's OK, as the steps are the same.

Because we wanted to test how many cameras could be added successfully, three webcams were connected to the Pi, but we will only use two of them in the final project implementation. For this system configuration, we installed:

- **WebCam 1**: This is a Microsoft LifeCam Studio camera connected to the Pi motherboard USB port. The development system has a maximum of 1.2 Ampere supplied from the Amazon Basics USB hub. We decided to only plug in one camera to the motherboard USB connections to ensure it was well within the power supply rating.

- **WebCam 2**: This is a Microsoft LifeCam Studio camera connected to a port on the USB hub.

- **WebCam 3**: This is a Logitech Webcam Pro 9000 camera connected to a port on the USB hub.

- **Camera 4**: This is a PiNoIR compatible camera connected to the MIPI (CSI) port on the Pi motherboard.

Be careful when connecting your camera(s).The PiCam is very static-sensitive, and the cable and connectors need to be carefully handled to avoid damage. Also, be sure to power off the Pi when connecting the PiCam to the motherboard.

USB peripherals are designed to be plug-and-play with the power on; when you plug in the webcams, the OS will automatically sense their presence and load the appropriate driver.

To verify that the webcams are connected and the driver loaded, open a Terminal session and perform the following steps:

1. Type `lsusb`, which will return a list of the USB devices present.

2. Type `lsusb -t`, which will show the connection tree for the USB devices.

3. Type `sudo find /dev/vid*`, which will return the active driver-supported devices related to video; depending on the number of cameras, you will see `/dev/video0`, `/dev/video1`, and so on.

The following is a screenshot of a system; there are three cameras connected as devices `004`, `009`, and `010`. You can view their position in the USB connection tree. There are also some audio device interfaces that appear as devices in the `lsusb -t` tree listing. These are the microphones in the webcams; we will use them later in the book.

Most USB web cameras are designed to a standard called **USB Video Class (UVC)**, which is automatically detected by the Raspbian OS. If your cameras do not show up as **videox**, where **x** is the logical device number using the **uvcvideo** driver, then you will need to find and load suitable drivers to use these devices.

Solving these types of hardware and driver issues are beyond the scope of this book, so make sure that your cameras are recognized correctly as UVC devices (they are represented by an entry in `/dev/video`) and are automatically detected before you continue.

# Testing camera capability

Let's begin testing the camera's capability. To do this, we can use a simple utility called **luvcview** to acquire images from the camera. We need to collect enough information to make a decision about the following elements of our design:

- Image resolution for captured images
- Frames per second (**fps**) to capture images

There are no absolute numbers available from any camera utility, but we can infer a base capability with some very simple tests. The utility (**luvcview**) reads from the camera and renders to the screen as fast as possible, which is up to the maximum frame rate of the camera (typically 30 fps). This read/render task will use all the available CPU resources it needs or can get. To install the luvcview utility, open a Terminal session and type `sudo apt-get install -y luvcview`.

Test each of your webcam cameras to determine how fast the cameras are at each potential image resolution and what frame rate you might achieve for the project. To determine the potential resolutions and an approximate frame rate to read from camera and render to screen, perform the following steps:

1. At the command prompt, type `luvcview -d /dev/video0 -L > /home/pi/vid0-char.txt`. The utility will print out the palettes, frame sizes, and frame rates supported by the camera and write it to a text file.
2. Use the File Manager application to find the text file
3. Use the Leafpad editor application to open the text file and see the image sizes and frame rates that the camera can be programmed to deliver. For each of the palettes, the resolution is usually the same but the frame rate may vary.

In the following screenshot, the typical image options available for MJPEG for our Microsoft Lifecam are shown:

```
pi@raspberrypi: ~                                    _  □ ×
File  Edit  Tabs  Help
{ pixelformat = 'MJPG', description = 'MJPEG' }
{ discrete: width = 640, height = 480 }
     Time interval between frame: 1/30, 1/20, 1/15, 1/10, 2/15,
{ discrete: width = 1920, height = 1080 }
     Time interval between frame: 1/30, 1/20, 1/15, 1/10, 2/15,
{ discrete: width = 1280, height = 720 }
     Time interval between frame: 1/30, 1/20, 1/15, 1/10, 2/15,
{ discrete: width = 960, height = 544 }
     Time interval between frame: 1/30, 1/20, 1/15, 1/10, 2/15,
{ discrete: width = 800, height = 448 }
     Time interval between frame: 1/30, 1/20, 1/15, 1/10, 2/15,
{ discrete: width = 640, height = 360 }
     Time interval between frame: 1/30, 1/20, 1/15, 1/10, 2/15,
{ discrete: width = 800, height = 600 }
     Time interval between frame: 1/30, 1/20, 1/15, 1/10, 2/15,
{ discrete: width = 432, height = 240 }
     Time interval between frame: 1/30, 1/20, 1/15, 1/10, 2/15,
{ discrete: width = 352, height = 288 }
     Time interval between frame: 1/30, 1/20, 1/15, 1/10, 2/15,
{ discrete: width = 176, height = 144 }
     Time interval between frame: 1/30, 1/20, 1/15, 1/10, 2/15,
{ discrete: width = 320, height = 240 }
     Time interval between frame: 1/30, 1/20, 1/15, 1/10, 2/15,
{ discrete: width = 160, height = 120 }
     Time interval between frame: 1/30, 1/20, 1/15, 1/10, 2/15,
```

# Viewing CPU resource for the luvcview application

In the **luvcview** window, you will see the video output from the first camera. The frame rate achieved is shown in the title bar. You can also see that the CPU indicator in the taskbar shows 100 percent utilization, which is an aggregate of all tasks running on the computer.

To get a better view of the CPU usage for just this application, perform the following steps:

1.  At the command prompt, type `luvcview -d /dev/video0 -s 640x480`.
2.  Start **Task Manager**.
3.  Click on the **CPU%** column to order tasks by CPU usage.
4.  Look for **luvcview** in CPU usage; it will probably be in the range of 20–50 percent and be the task consuming the most resources. This is the amount of CPU resource being used or all that is available due to other tasks running.

While these percentages are not very accurate, they do give you an approximate idea of the frames per second (fps) that can be achieved. For example, a Microsoft LifeCam Studio camera @ 640 x 480 resolution consumes about 46 percent CPU at approximately 5 fps on a single-processor Pi and about 40 percent CPU at 11 fps on the quad processor. In Task Manager, you will notice that **Xorg** consistently consumes 15–20 percent of the resources, while the X11 server renders the screen content.

The following screenshot shows luvcview's CPU usage in the **Task Manager** application:

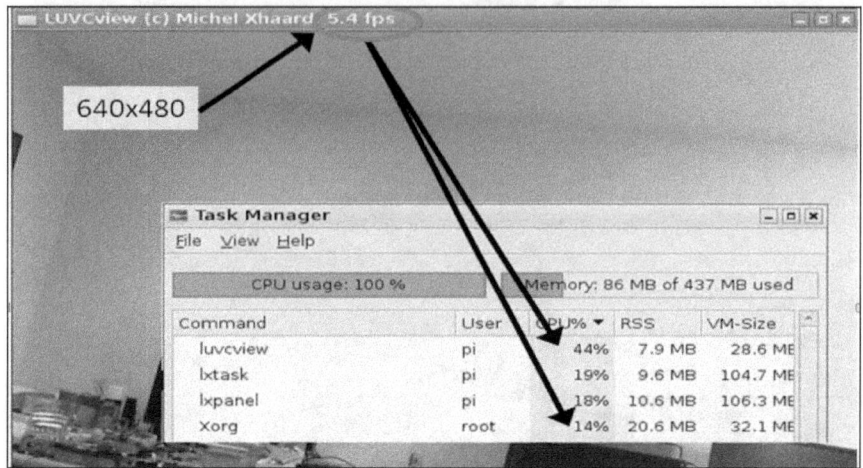

As shown in the preceding image, we built a camera table shown below that compares the fps and CPU percentage for two image resolutions. Try making a similar table for your cameras.

| Camera | fps@320 x 240 | 320 x 240 CPU percent | fps@640 x 480 | 640 x 480 CPU percent |
|---|---|---|---|---|
| MS LifeCam Studio | 30 (13) | 60 (35) | 11 (5) | 40 (45) |
| Logitech Quickcam Pro | 30 (14) | 75 (33) | 12 (6) | 49 (45) |
| PiCam/PiNoIR (Raspivid1) | 30 | <10 | 30 | <10 |
| PiCam/PiNoIR (motion-mmal2) | 10 selected | 25 | 10 selected | 25 |

The numbers in parentheses shown in the table above are for the single-processor Pi.

The PiCam has built-in applications that support it in Raspbian Wheezy. These applications control the camera through a direct API and are non-UVC video compliant (see Raspivid in the preceding table). Since they perform the bulk of the video acquisition task in the hardware, the CPU resources used are very low.

Visit `http://www.raspberrypi.org/documentation/raspbian/applications/camera.md` for comprehensive details on the application configuration and use.

Open source contributors have built components to allow **RaspiCam** to be controlled by an application called **motion** and directly by Python. This version of motion is specially built to support the Picam. This add-on capability still does not make the RaspiCam **uvcvideo**-compliant but does allow flexible acquisition and motion sensing using PiCam. The motion software proved unreliable to use with PiNoIR because the lighting impacted the movement detection. So, the security camera design did not use this software solution, but it was used to acquire the table information shown earlier.

Your cameras should run continuously without errors; both read and sync errors may occur on some cameras. If the test application stops reading from the camera, or if the display becomes corrupted, do not use the camera. For example, in testing the Logitech Quickcam Pro, the display would break up after several hours of operation. Sometimes, it would recover and regain synchronization, but at other times it was required to stop the application and restart to correct the problem. We, therefore, used the Microsoft Lifecam Studio camera in our project.

# Verifying the PiCam operation

In the following test process, you will see a full screen preview window of the PiCam video stream if your camera is working correctly. The video stream will be recorded at a default of 1920 x 1080 for 5 seconds and will be stored in your /home/pi directory as test.h264. The file size will be approximately 5MB. When the recording stops, you can see that the CPU indicator in the taskbar shows very low CPU utilization.

To verify the PiCam operation, you can use **Raspivid**, which is already installed in the Raspbian release, by performing the following steps in a Terminal session window:

1. At the command prompt, type sudo raspi-config

2. When raspi-config starts, select the option to enable the camera and then select **Finish** to exit the script and reboot the system. This will enable the use of the PiCam camera module.

3. Open the Terminal session window again (once your system has rebooted), and, at the command prompt, type raspivid -o test.h264 -t 5000. Once the capture has completed in this and the following process steps, examine the video file size produced.

The video will be recorded at a default of 1920 x 1080 for 5 seconds and will be stored in your pi directory as test.h264; it should be about 5 MB in size. You can also see that the CPU indicator in the taskbar (when the recording stops) shows very low CPU utilization.

4. At the command prompt, type `raspivid -o test.h264 -t 60000` to record 60 seconds @1920 x 1080, and the file size, depending on content and compression, should be about 65–75 MB. This would require about 4.5 GB of storage space per hour of video content!

5. At the command prompt, type `raspivid -o test.h264 -t 60000 -w 1920 -h 1080 -p 0,0,640,480`.

> The changes to the command line here allow the size and position of the preview window to be altered. If you leave out the –p option and add an –n option, there will be no preview window at all.

6. To display the recorded file at the command prompt, type `omxplayer ./test.h264`.

> The omxplayer utility is able to use the H264 hardware acceleration features in the Raspberry Pi SOC to play the video with very low CPU utilization.

7. Use File Manager to delete the video files you just acquired.

8. Ensure that **Moving files to the rubbish bin** (under **Edit/Preferences**) is turned off to prevent deleted files from continuing to require filesystem space or use *Shift + Del* to immediately delete the files.

# Controlling data storage for video

Next, you need to understand the implications and methods of storing video security information without consuming too much space in the filesystem.

When designing a security camera system, you must always be aware of data storage requirements.

The Pi is constrained by the capacity of the SD card. We could increase the size of the SD card to 16 GB, 32 GB, 64 GB, or even 128 GB (with increased cost) to provide more space for video, but even with 128 GB of space this represents only 24 hours of PiCam high-resolution video.

Reducing the frame rate or resolution is one way to reduce your data storage needs. The frame rate and resolution must, however, be high enough to ensure that we reliably detect movement as someone passes into the camera's field of view, but low enough to limit storage space requirements. At 1 frame per second for example, it might just be possible for an Olympic athlete to sprint through the camera's field of view and be missed completely.

If the filesystem fills to maximum capacity, the OS will stop working. Let's address data storage for the security camera system by providing limited storage space that does not interfere with the normal operating system and user files.

If you remember the installation process in *Chapter 1, Getting Started with Raspberry Pi*, you selected Raspbian and a 512 MB data partition. It's time to explain how that data partition was configured in the system. The plan is to use this partition for storage of captured video files.

To see how the disk (SD card) is laid out, we use a utility called **GParted**. This provides a visual of the partitions, their sizes, and the installed filesystem on the SD card. The following steps show you how to install and use gparted:

1. At a Terminal session, type `sudo apt-get -y install gparted`.

2. Once installed, you can start the utility from **Menu | Preferences | Gparted**. You have to enter your account password to start the utility.

The following screenshot shows the GParted screenshot of the system:

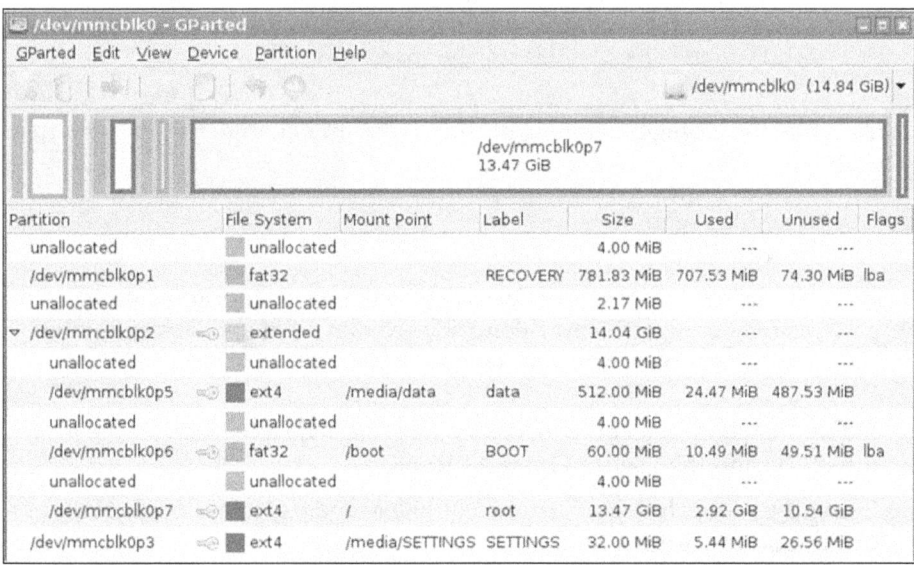

Note that, in the GParted image from our system we have a 16 GB SD card and the major extended partition on the SD card is `/dev/mmcblk0p2`, where `p2` indicates the partition number. Within that partition, several other partitions are defined:

- `/dev/mmcblk0p7`: This is the ext4 system root partition
- `/dev/mmcblk0p6`: This is the FAT32 boot partition

- `/dev/mmcblk0p5`: This is the ext4 512 MB data partition

> You may notice that the first partition labeled `/dev/mmcblk0p1` is shown as the **RECOVERY** partition. This partition is actually a copy of the original NOOBS installation files from the installation in *Chapter 1, Getting Started with Raspberry Pi*. It's 700 MB in the current view, but if we had used NOOBS Lite, this partition would only be about 75 MB, allowing another 600 MB of space for the operating system.

The partition manager allows the creation, deletion, expansion, mount, and unmount of partitions. We have only used it to view the partition data; you can read the Man (OS Help System) pages to learn more about how to use this powerful tool.

During the install process, the data partition was mounted at a point in the root file system named `/media/data`, and we can use File Manager to see the contents.

> If you rebuild your system from the **RECOVERY** partition at any time, the data may be renamed `data0`, `data1` and so on. This does not cause any problems other than the fact that you may need to alter any URI you use to access this storage space.

Now, let's create the storage area for our video files and change the ownership and group to pi:

1. Open File Manager.

> By default, File Manager opens only with user privileges (pi is the current user), and we are going to need root privileges for some of the next steps because **/media** and **/media/data** belong to root.

2. In File Manager, select the directory tree **/media**, right-click on the **/data** directory, and then select **Open As Root**.

3. Using the root privileged instance of File Manager, select **Tools/Run a Command in Current Folder**.

4. In the **Run a Command** form, enter `mkdir video` and click on **OK**.

5. Select **Tools | Run a Command in Current Folder** again.

6. In the **Run a Command** form, enter `chown pi:  video`, and click on **OK**.

Here is an alternative process to set ownership:

1. In File Manager, right-click on the **video** folder and select **Properties**, and then, in the properties dialog, select **Permissions**.

2. Currently, the folder Owner and Group is set to root, set both entries to **pi**.

3. Click on **Ok** on the properties dialog.

4. Click **Ok** on the permissions confirmation dialog to finalize the change. The video folder now belongs to the user pi.

 Notice in File Manager that, if you highlight the **/media** folder, the total space available is 14.1 GB, and if you highlight the **/media/data/video** folder, the total space is about 500 MB. While the **/media/data** folder is part of the file system, it is permanently constrained to approximately 512 MB and cannot overflow this space limit.

The following image summarizes the preceding steps performed:

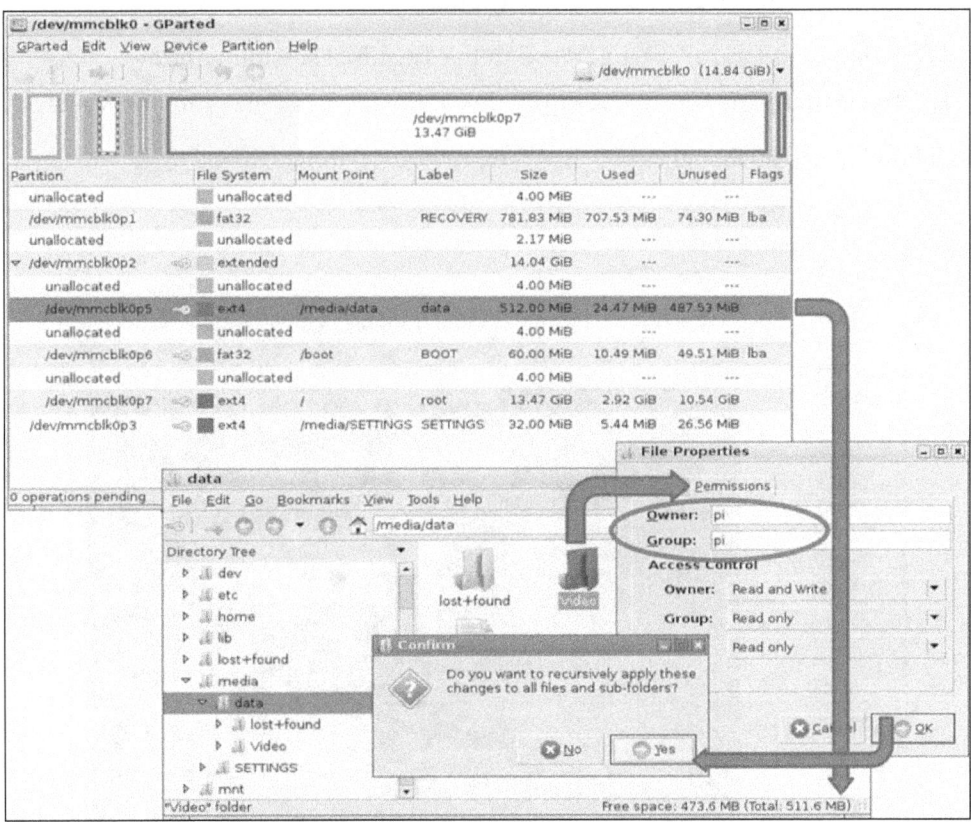

# Testing the data storage limit

To test that our storage limit does exactly what we want it to do, let's fill the folder with a video data stream as shown in the following list of steps:.

1. In File Manager, focus on the **/media.data/video** folder and open a Terminal session window using **Tools/Open Current Folder in Terminal**.

2. Type `raspivid-o /media/data/video/test.h264 -t 0 -n -v` to start continuous acquisition from the **RaspiCam**, writing to our size-constrained folder with no preview screen and verbose output.

As can be seen in the image that follows, video acquisition ran until it reached 473.6 MB, which is very close to our 512 MB size limit, and then resulted in write errors.

While it would be nice for the application to close down gracefully when it can no longer write, this current result neatly prevents overconsumption of storage space. A well-written application would capture the error and stop the `raspivid` process.

Peform the following steps to delete the test file:

1. To stop `raspivid`, enter *Ctrl + C* in the Terminal session window.

2. To clean up after our test, simply delete the file `test.h264` in File Manager.

The following screenshot encapsulates the previously shown steps:

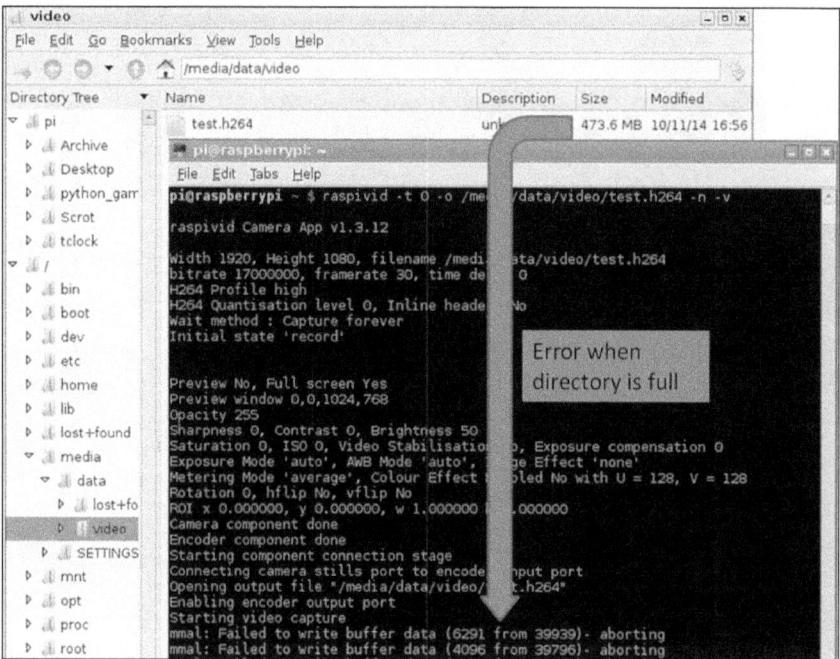

We now have a storage area for our video files that is size-constrained and, while it's only 512 MB, it's big enough for testing purposes. If you wish to use your own design for a security camera system, you could increase video storage space with one of the following methods:

- Reinstall your system on a larger SD card (16 GB or more) without selecting the 512 MB install option. Post install, create a partition of a more suitable-sized portion of the SD card using the Gnome Partition Editor (GParted). Depending on when you do this, you might have to shrink `/dev/mmcblk0p7`, which is the ext4 system filesystem root partition, to provide free space in which to create your new **/data** partition.

- Install USB storage with sufficient space for your video files. The Raspbian OS will auto-mount a USB storage key or USB-based hard drive on **/media**, and, if it has a label, use that as the directory name. If there is no label, it will create a numerical reference.

> In one of those little quirks that can make your head spin, if the partition editor is running, the OS will not auto-mount removable USB storage keys. Make sure you are not running the tool if you want auto-mount to work.

# Project 1 – Running raspivid as a background service

Let's set up raspivid so that, as it runs in the background, we can simply send a message to the process to stop or start video acquisition. This setup can also work for taking snapshot still images with raspistill too.

The script we will create allows you to easily control rapsivid from the command line. The command line in the script that instantiates the raspivid process looks like this:

```
sudo raspivid -w 800 -h 600 -i pause -n -o
/media/data/video/test%03d.h264 -sg 10000 -s -t 0 &
```

| Code | Description |
|------|-------------|
| `raspivid` | This could also be `raspistill` or `raspiyuv` with different options. For more details, visit `http://www.raspberrypi.org/documentation/usage/camera/raspicam/README.md`. |

| Code | Description |
|------|-------------|
| `-w 800`<br>`-h 600` | This sets the height and width of the captured image. |
| `-i pause` | This starts the playback in a paused state. |
| `-n` | This sets the no-preview window. If you want preview, you can remove this flag and add either `-f` for a fullscreen preview or the `-p <x,y,w,h>` option to set a preview window size. |
| `-o /media/data/`<br>`video/test%02d.`<br>`h264` | This sets the path to capture the filename. `%0Xd`, which sets the numerical count. It starts at 1 and, if the process stops and restarts, it will start at 1 again. If the count reaches a maximum, it will roll over and start again at 1. |
| `-sg 10000` | This is the number in milliseconds. The capture file will change every X ms, so in this case it is 10 seconds.<br><br>Use `-sp` to split the file on each record event signal. |
| `-s -t 0` | `-s` enables the use of the `-usr1` signal to toggle recording/pause.<br><br>`-t 0` is required when using `-s`, or raspivid will unload when it pauses. |
| `&` | This detaches the process so that you can continue to use the command prompt |

There are many more optional parameters you could use to configure video acquisition with raspivid.

 Read the camera documentation details at
`http://www.raspberrypi.org/documentation/`
`raspbian/applications/camera.md`.

# Project 1a – Creating a Bash script to drive raspivid

In this project, we will use a small Bash shell script using the command line shown to instantiate raspivid as a root process. The script will only start raspivid if there is no instance already running, and it will start the process in a paused mode. Command-line parameters will let us start or pause recording and unload the process.

The following steps show you how to get started:

1.  Open File Manager and create a directory called camera in `/home/pi` for our work.

2.  Download the `picam.sh` file from the `Chapter 3` folder at `http://1drv.ms/1ysAxkl`; make it executable and ensure that the owner is pi.

3.  Open `picam.sh` in the Leafpad editor.

The Bash script code for `picam.sh` is fully documented in the file; however, here is a quick overview of some of the important elements of the script:

*   A case statement is used to allow the user to execute the file specifying one of the five command actions as a parameter. We can `Load`, `Quit`, `Record`, `Pause`, or show `Status`.

*   The script creates a variable called `pidnum` and a file, called `picam_state.txt` to allow checks for the process presence and its current state (paused, recording, and so on)

*   The command line that instantiates **raspivid** captures video data at 800 x 600 with each video stream being 10 seconds long. The filename created is `test%2d.h264` so, after 99 files are acquired, the acquisition will start to overwrite older files. Since the 10-second video captures are typically no larger than 3.5 MB, the `/media/data/video` directory will never fill, but the captured data is limited to around 350 MB or 16 minutes in total.

*   There is a commented-out command line that you can try that shows a 320 x 240 preview window and captures video data continuously into a single file with the capture time set by record/pause.

# Testing the picam.sh script

To better understand the operation of the `picam.sh` script, perform the following steps:

1.  Open a command session and type `./picam.sh` at the command line to ensure that it is working (it should show you help).

2.  Test all the options, load, quit, record, and pause, and ensure the acquired files are being stored in `/media/data/video`.

3. After reviewing the documentation, try the following modifications to the command in the script that starts raspivid:

   1. Remove the `-n` flag on the raspivid command line and replace it with `-p 0,0,320,240`. This will show a small preview window in the top-left corner of your display when raspivid is running. The preview will be there whether or not raspivid is recording.

   2. Remove the `-sg 10000` parameter and use the `-sp` flag. This will start a new file each time you start recording instead of recording many 10-second files.

You now have quite a useful script tool to control the PiCam video acquisition from the command line, and one last thing we might like to test is running the script automatically each time the computer boots.

During the talking clock project in *Chapter 2, Configuring the Raspberry Pi Desktop and Software*, we started the script using a `crontab` entry called `@reboot`. Unfortunately, this option won't work for raspivid. A `crontab` entry for `picam.sh` will start the process, but you will be unable to send the signal `-usr1` used to turn the recording on and off. The reason behind this is a little complicated, but it boils down to processes being created in process groups. Within a group, you can send all signals to the processes, but you cannot send all signals across groups.

There is an easy solution to this problem; we will add the script to `/etc/rc.local`. This system script file runs automatically each time the computer exits to a multiuser runtime level, such as the pi user logon that starts the desktop processes. Since all subsequent processes are in the same process tree, the `-usr1` signals can get through.

Perform the following steps to add the startup instruction to load raspivid to `rc.local`:

1. Use File Manager with root access and browse to `/etc`.

2. Right-click on the `rc.local` file and open it in Leafpad.

3. Type `/home/pi/picam.sh load &` on the line before the last entry `exit 0`, as shown in the following listing:

```
#!/bin/sh -e
#
# rc.local
#
# This script is executed at the end of each multiuser runlevel.
# Make sure that the script will "exit 0" on success or any other
# value on error.
#
```

```
# In order to enable or disable this script just change the
execution
# bits.
#
# By default this script does nothing.

# Print the IP address
_IP=$(hostname -I) || true
if [ "$_IP" ]; then
  printf "My IP address is %s\n" "$_IP"
fi

# Enter this line of text
/home/pi/camera/picam.sh load &

exit 0
```

4. Save the file and reboot the Pi.

5. Use Task Manager to verify that the raspivid process has started and that the record and pause functions work.

6. To remove the auto-start feature, simply delete the relevant line of the script from rc.local and reboot the Pi.

# Project 1b – Creating a movement detector with a USB camera

For our security system to record video only when there is action, we need to detect movement. One application that does this very reliably is an application called **motion**.

There is a version of motion that will work with a PiCam camera, but if we use PiCam to acquire high-resolution images at high frame rates, the CPU resources required by motion will increase significantly. Instead, we will reduce the CPU usage as much as possible by detecting movement at very slow frame rates (2 fps is normally quite adequate) and use a USB webcam to do this. By separating the high-quality, high frame-rate video acquisition task from the movement detection task, we can achieve both reliable operation and low overall CPU usage.

First, let's install the motion application on the computer:

Using File Manager, browse to /home/pi/camera and then enter *F4* (a shortcut to open a Terminal session with this folder as the working directory).

1. At the command prompt, type sudo apt-get -y install motion

2. At the command prompt type, sudo cp /etc/motion/motion.conf motion.ref

3. Open /home/pi/camera/motion.ref in Leafpad.

The motion utility is very flexible and can acquire video and still images with various options for timing and movement detection as defined in the motion.ref file. The motion.conf (the one in the /etc folder) file describes the configuration selections and is read when the motion executable is started, unless you specify a unique configuration file to be used. There is good documentation on motion in the **man** pages, but for comprehensive coverage, visit the motion homepage at http://www.lavrsen.dk/foswiki/bin/view/Motion/WebHome or file:///usr/share/doc/motion/motion_guide.html.

The documentation for motion directs you to create a unique motion.conf file for your purposes. We just created a motion.ref file to aid in reviewing the configuration options and will create a much smaller motion.conf.test configuration file for testing. The absolute filename is unimportant, but renaming it keeps it unique to our project. Most of the options in the motion.ref configuration file have default values. Read through the partial list of options shown in the following code. Note that this is a subset of the values that are not set to default values but are required to be set for our unique motion detection task. The following is the configuration file for motion:

```
############################################################
#Daemon
############################################################
daemon off
############################################################
#Capture device options
############################################################
videodevice /dev/video0    #defines the video device we capture
from
# Pallette is MJPG
v4l2_palette 2    #defines the output file format
# Image width (pixels). Valid range: Camera dependent, default:
352
width 320  #x=320
# Image height (pixels). Valid range: Camera dependent, default:
288
```

```
height 240      #y=240
# Maximum number of frames to be captured per second.
# Valid range: 2-100. Default: 100 (almost no limit).
framerate 2     #capture at 2 frames per second
##########################################################
# Motion Detection Settings:
##########################################################
# Threshold for number of changed pixels in an image that
# triggers motion detection (default: 1500)
threshold 1500    #number of pixels for threshold

# Picture frames must contain motion at least the specified number
of frames
minimum_motion_frames 2          #number of frames to compare
##########################################################
# Target Directories and filenames For Images And Films
##########################################################
target_dir /media/data/video  #where to store video files
##########################################################
# External Commands, Warnings and Logging:
##########################################################

# Command to be executed when an event starts. (default: none)
;on_event_start /home/pi/camera/security.sh record

# Command to be executed when an event ends after a period of no
motion
;on_event_end /home/pi/camera/security.sh pause
```

As noted in the configuration file elements shown in the preceding code, the features and options we need for our project are as follows:

- The video must be captured from /dev/video0 with 320 x 240 resolution at 2 fps

- Motion must occur in two consecutive video frames with at least a 1500-pixel difference required to be registered as a motion event. Always capture at least 10 frames for a motion event.

- Still images are not captured along with video.

- The FFMPEG video is captured, stamped with date and time to the /media/data/video directory.

- The HTTP server is started for both control and images. The default image output is 1 fps (this setting is not shown in the listing shown previously).

- Trigger commands are used to start and stop the PiCam camera's high-quality, high-frame-rate acquisition. Note that these settings are commented out in the configuration preceding listing and in the file you download (we will enable them later).

You can create your own copy of `motion.ref`, delete all the default values, and save it as `/home/pi/camera/motion.conf.test` if you wish to experiment. Since not all the values you need to set are shown in the aforementioned listing, the complete `motion.conf.test` file is available for download from the `Chapter 3` folder at `http://1drv.ms/1ysAxkl`.

# Test the webcam installation

To test that your webcam is correctly installed on your computer, and to verify the driver is loaded, perform the following test steps:

From a command prompt, perform the following steps:

1. Type `lsusb` to verify that the USB camera was detected.
2. Type `ls /dev/vid*`, which should show that you have `/dev/video0`.
3. Type `fswebcam test.jpg` to acquire a test image.
4. In File Manager. right-click on the file and view the image using Image Viewer.

To test the `motion.conf.test` file you downloaded or created, perform the following steps:

1. In File Manager, browse to `/media/data/video`.
2. Delete all the files in the video directory so that you can see what files motion app adds.

From a command prompt, type the motion `-n -c /home/pi/camera/motion.conf.test` to start the application. It will print out the status details of the configuration. You should see information about the camera, the driver used, the video size, and the starting of the web server and the command web service.

From your desktop, start the web browser on the taskbar:

1. Type 127.0.0.1:8080 or localhost:8080 in the URL address bar. If the web server is running correctly, you should see a title for Motion 3.2.12 running with one thread.

2. Click on **All** and you will see the Thread 0 commands you can perform from the website.

3. Click on **action** and then on **snapshot**

   This should cause a *snapshot.jpg file to be written to the /media/data/ video directory. You can view this with **Image Viewer**. Also, at this level, you can quit the motion application, which will shut down the process in an orderly fashion.

 Note that this web-based control for **motion** gives you all you need to build a remote, motion-controlled, USB-based still and video camera.

4. Start a new browser tab in the web browser.

5. Type 127.0.0.1:8081 in the URL address bar. If the web server is running correctly, you should see the image from the web camera being refreshed at approximately 1 fps. If you move your hand in front of the web camera or walk back and forth in the field of view, you will create motion events. As a result, <dateandtime>.avi video files are created.

 The motion application buffers a considerable amount of data in memory, so it may take several movements to cause a file to be written. This should be a <dateandtime>.avi file, which may not be very large initially, but should grow as you move in and out of the camera's field of view and generate more events.

As you move in and out of the camera's field of view, the movements recorded are added to a single file. If you keep moving, it just continues to accumulate data. After no movement is detected for 10 seconds, the event ends, and a new movement event file is created on the next movement detection. When you have accumulated 50 KB or so of data, you can either enter *Ctrl + C* in the command window where you started the motion or type All - action - quit in the website command interface.

If you view the website provided by the motion application HTTP server at `127.0.0.1:8081` using the **Epiphany** web browser, it correctly shows the 1 fps image changes. The web server generates a stream in the **multipart jpeg format** (**mjpeg**). You cannot watch the stream with most browsers. Only certain versions of Netscape and Mozilla Firefox browsers can view the mjpeg stream, but you often have to refresh the page once to get the streaming going. Internet Explorer cannot show the mjpeg stream. For public viewing, this is not very useful. There exists a java applet called **Cambozola**, which enables any Java-capable browser to show the stream. To enable the feature to a broad audience, you should use this applet or something similar. Read the following for more information:

```
http://www.lavrsen.dk/foswiki/bin/view/Motion/
WebcamServer
```

On the Raspberry Pi, you can use **omxplayer** or the Epiphany web browser to view the video `*.avi` files that the motion application writes to the data-storage area.

There is one last problem to address that you might experience with the video produced by a USB webcam. The web camera may often readjust focus when a target enters the field of view since most cameras automatically do this. This change of focus can erroneously produce what appears to be a massive change in the pixels and therefore trigger a motion event.

Motion has entries in the configuration file that allow for camera brightness, contrast, and hue to be controlled, but it does not have any way to control the autofocus function. Luckily for us, there is a utility called **uvcdynctrl** for cameras that are compliant with **uvcvideo** that provides this control.

To install uvcdynctrl for the uvcvideo utility:

1. From a command prompt, type `sudo apt-get -y install uvcdynctrl`.

2. In the command prompt, type `uvcdynctrl -c -d /dev/video0` to print out the controllable parameters for the camera. Take note of the string value to address autofocus; on our Microsoft camera, it was `Focus, Auto`.

3. From the command prompt, type `uvcdynctrl -g "Focus, Auto" -d /dev/video0` to print out the current value of this parameter. Remember to use this string for your camera.

4. From the command prompt, type `uvcdynctrl -s "Focus, Auto" -d /dev/video0 0` to set `Focus, Auto` to zero, turning the feature off. The camera will remain in this fixed focus configuration until it is turned off and will have to be reconfigured each time it is turned on. By adding this command to any script you create, you can prevent the camera from autofocusing.

# A final word on resolution and frame rate for movement detection

Motion uses a detection algorithm that is relatively simple. It keeps a buffer of the number of frames required to designate movement detection, applies any filtering, and then calculates the number of pixels changed between frames.

The frame size sets the number of pixels that the software must scan, and the frame rate sets the time gap between the frames. For many of the standard image sizes the following table shows the number of pixels per frame. For a comparison to take place, the software has to scan twice this number of pixels since we used two frames to define the movement detector event. Here's the aforementioned table:

| Resolution | 320*240 | 352*288 | 640*480 | 800*600 | 1920*1080 |
|---|---|---|---|---|---|
| **Number of Pixels** | 768 k | 1 M | 3 M | 5 M | 20 M |

The preceding table explains why the CPU resources can be so rapidly used up when you acquire images above 352 x 288. The reason we suggested 320 x 240 (353 x 288 is viable too) is that it's a relatively useful image size, and the smallest CPU load.

The frame rate was selected at the lowest possible value of 2 fps. If the movement you detected is people crossing an area, it is unlikely their speed will be much over 2 m/s. Depending on the field of view of your camera and the distance to the target motion, you only need one frame to register a major change in pixels. If traffic is moving very rapidly and the target is small, you might need to go to 3 fps. You can experiment to find the right setting for your application.

If you want to use higher frame rates or larger image sizes, this is a good time to consider fitting a heatsink to your CPU and bumping up the clock rate. Go to http://www.raspberrypi.org/introducing-turbo-mode-up-to-50-more-performance-for-free/ for more details. Strictly speaking, you don't need a heatsink if you use the turbo mode. However, if the temperature of your CPU/memory rises above a trigger point, the clock rate will be reduced automatically.

# Project 2 – Combining the webcam movement detector and the PiCam camera

Now that we have a working PiCam script and know which configuration details are needed to enable motion movement detection, we can update the Bash script from *Project 1a – Creating a Bash script to drive raspivid* to include this motion detector feature. So, we need to enable actions in the motion configuration file to start and pause recording using a script.

Here is a preview of what is added to the new security.sh script:

- For the load option, the command lines to start motion are added and the USB camera is set to a fixed focus

- For the quit option, a command line is added to kill motion

- For the motion configuration file, the following events are enabled:

    ○ A motion-detect event that turns on PiCam recording

    ○ An end-of-movement event that pauses PiCam recording

Since the script file is now over 100 lines long, it would be quite a chore to type in the changes. To get the new file with the changes added as described in the previous list of points, perform the following steps:

1. Download the security.sh script to the camera directory from the Chapter 3 folder at http://1drv.ms/1ysAxkl.

2. Ensure that, when you download the file, you set the properties to ownership by pi, and that it is marked as an executable.

3. Using Leafpad, compare picam.sh to security.sh and notice the changes made to the load, quit, and status commands to add the new functionality.

 Be sure to read each hash mark (#) comment in any script code you download as they summarize the intent of a line or section of code. You could even potentially remove the .sh extension from the file when you download it as this was only to remind you during development that it was a script file. The shebang at the beginning of the file is all that is actually required to ensure Bash is used to interpret the script.

4. Using Leafpad, enable the action parameters in `motion.conf.test` by removing the `;` character that comments out the lines, as shown in the following code:

```
# Command to be executed when an event starts. (default:
none)
on_event_start /home/pi/camera/security.sh record >
/dev/null

# Command to be executed when an event ends after a period
of no motion
on_event_end /home/pi/camera/security.sh pause > /dev/null
```

5. Using File Manager, delete all the files in `/media/data/video`, so you can easily see the files being added by raspivid and motion.

6. Using File Manager, browse to `/home/pi/camera` and then press *F4* (a shortcut to open a Terminal session with this folder as the working directory).

7. From File Manager, use **Tools | Open Current Folder in Terminal** to start a command-line session.

8. In the command-line session, type `./security quit`, which will ensure that neither raspivid nor motion are running.

9. In the command-line session, type `./security load` to instantiate both raspivid and motion. You should see messages showing both applications start.

Now we have a security camera system working with two cameras. Using this setup for a complete day accumulated about 200 MB of video files of traffic in and out of my office. In a non-work environment, for example monitoring access to a bedroom, this system could run for several days, even in a restricted 512 MB partition.

Depending on the application you have, you may need to consider fine-tuning `motion.conf.test` to suit your particular needs, as follows:

- To extend or change the functionality of your security system, consider the following: adding directory size checks so that a warning is sent (e-mail) or the older files are deleted if the video storage directory approaches full.

- Increase the number of movement-detecting cameras to protect multiple entrance points (doors and windows). This requires the use of multiple threads (one thread per camera) for motion, so you need to read the documentation in detail.

- Send the small `.avi` files via e-mail as intrusion alerts.

# Project 3 – Creating a simple Python GUI for the security application

We will use a very simple Python application that presents two buttons. One button loads and unloads the raspivid and motion application services, and the second starts and stops recording (irrespective of motion detection).

Python does not have any window-based functionality; it is purely text input by default. To provide a GUI, you have to provide extension libraries and, in this case, we will use a library called **tkinter**. In the code, we will use tkinter to define the two buttons and will use the OS library to call out to our existing shell script to perform the needed actions.

Perform the following steps to create a Python GUI for your security script:

1. Install `python-tk` using the `apt-get` command.

2. Create a blank file in `/home/pi/camera` called `buttons.py`.

3. Set the permissions for the file to be executable and ensure the ownership is set to the user pi.

4. Double-click on IDLE 3 to open the Python development shell and use **File | Open** to open `buttons.py` in the editor window. If you use the editor, then it will catch mistakes you might make where Leafpad would not.

5. Type the following code (or download the `buttons.py` file from the `Chapter 3` folder at `http://1drv.ms/1ysAxkl`):

```python
#!/usr/bin/python3

import tkinter as tk
import os

# the defines below are the code that is activated on a button
press
def button1():
    if buttonone["text"] == "Load":
        os.system( "/home/pi/camera/security.sh quit" )
        os.system( "/home/pi/camera/security.sh load" )
        # switch to Quit
        buttonone["text"] = "Quit"
    else:
        os.system( "/home/pi/camera/security.sh quit" )
        # reset to Load
        buttonone["text"] = "Load"

def button2():
    if buttontwo["text"] == "Record":
```

```
        os.system( "/home/pi/camera/security.sh record" )
        # switch to Pause
        buttontwo["text"] = "Pause"
    else:
        os.system( "/home/pi/camera/security.sh pause" )
        # reset to Record
        buttontwo["text"] = "Record"

# Define tkinter window and title for the window
mywin = tk.Tk()
mywin.title("Security Camera")

# Define buttons
buttonone = tk.Button( text="Load", width=18, command=button1)
buttonone.pack(padx=18, pady=0)

buttontwo = tk.Button( text="Record", width=18, command=button2)
buttontwo.pack(padx=18, pady=0)

# Start the window message loop
mywin.mainloop()
```

The following screenshot shows the **raspvid** process in **Task Manager**, and the motion that is detected and saved as a file in **File Manager**:

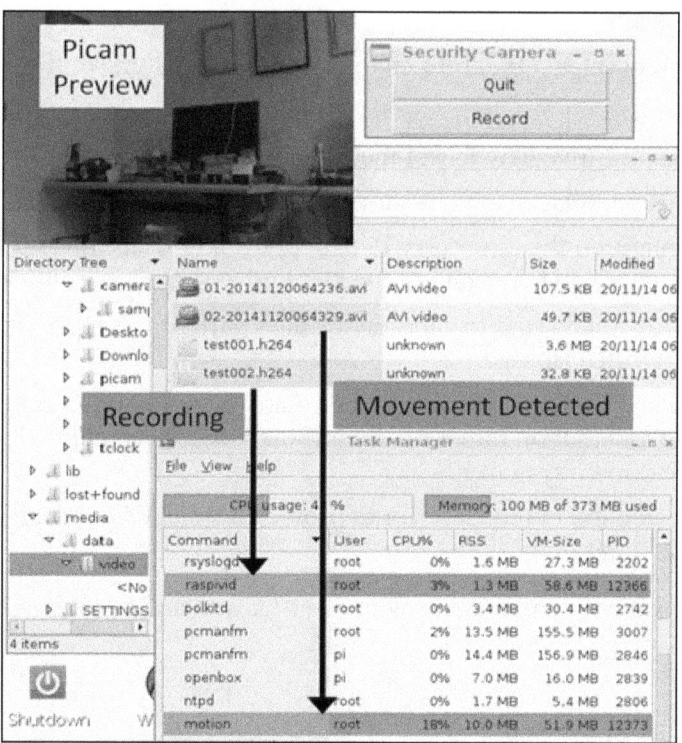

Within the IDLE 3 development environment, you can test the Python code:

1.  In the editor window, use **Run | Run Module** to start the program.

2.  The two-button GUI should appear, and you are able to **Load/Quit** and **Record/Pause** the security camera system.

3.  If you exit the IDLE 3 environment, you can start the `buttons.py` application from a command-line session or double-click and select **execute** from within File Manager.

While creating a comprehensive GUI application may be challenging, you can see from the `button.py` application that it is possible to easily create a relatively simple window-based controller. We will cover the use of this Python development environment in much more detail in later chapters.

The preceding image shows the resource usage for movement detection and video acquisition. Notice that **raspivid** is using a very low amount of CPU resources, and motion considerably more. On the single-processor Raspberry Pi, you can expect motion to consume 10-20 percent of CPU resources depending on the video size used. On the quad processor Raspberry Pi, CPU resources may be only 4-10 percent.

# Summary

Now that we've completed the third chapter, let's review some of the main tasks you learned to do:

*   You installed luvcview to test the camera's CPU usage

*   You used omxplayer to view video files

*   You configured the Raspberry Pi to support both webcam and PiCam video acquisition by installing the raspivid and motion utilities.

*   You installed GParted to validate the data partition used to manage file space for video storage

*   You created Bash shell scripts to automate raspivid and to combine raspivid and motion into a small but functional movement-triggered security camera system

*   You created the Python 3 script to provide a small GUI for the security camera.

In the next chapter, you will learn how to use VLC and audio devices to create an Internet radio.

# 4
# Raspberry Pi Audio Input and Output

While many home audio or TV systems include schemas such as Dolby Pro-Logic decoding for commercially produced media such as DVDs and CDs, Internet delivery of music has dramatically increased acceptance of simple stereo 2.1 sound. As a result of broader acceptance of stereo online music or podcast files, most radio stations have a streaming service to match their wireless broadcasts. After completing this chapter, you will be able to:

- Configure the Raspberry Pi to support an internal audio output device and add-on USB audio adapters
- Understand some of the limitations of sound playback devices on the Pi
- Install and configure USB sound devices under ALSA
- Install and configure VLC to play Internet-based "radio" streams
- Create a simple Python text interface to automate VLC
- Create and modify a fully-featured TKinter interface to implement a stereo Internet radio with a clock
- Capture sound from a microphone

# Audio quality and bandwidth

High-quality audio requires ever higher network bandwidth and computer CPU resources. When listening to Internet-based content, the network flow of data can become quite significant and, depending on the encoding schema, may require a higher allocation of CPU resources and, in addition, extremely low latency of data processing. Internet-based content streaming is available in a range of formats, with names such as **MP3, AAC(+), WMA, VORBIS, ASF, MMS, ASX, PLS, M3U**, that define the bandwidth and encoding schemes. The network bandwidth required for these streams may range from 32 Kbps for mono content to 640 Kbps for 5.1 multi-channel content.

# Audio capability on the Raspberry Pi

The Raspbian Wheezy installation on your Pi uses a software sound architecture called the **Advanced Linux Sound Architecture (ALSA)**. ALSA drivers allow dynamic sensing of audio devices as the system boots, or when a device is plugged in—if it is USB-based. The Pi hardware supports two sound output methods directly on the motherboard but does not have the microphone recording capability. This audio output capability is actually built into the Broadcom SOC. The inbuilt sound output channels supported are stereo headphone and line output on a 3.5 mm jack with combined composite video and digital audio over the HDMI connector.

The line output audio signal is generated using a **Pulse Width Modulation (PWM)** signal and is limited in audio bandwidth and power output. We recommend that you do not use low-impedance headphones (less than 16 Ohm) as the distortion and noise on the channels tends to increase. There are many high-impedance headphones available (32 Ohm and above), which provide adequate performance; however, they are limited to around 30 mW (milliwatts) per channel at maximum.

If the 3.5 mm output jack is fed into a PC-style sound system or a HiFi sound bar, or if the HDMI channel supports audio, then much higher output powers can be achieved.

# Limited headphone output

The PWM output stage for the stereo audio output uses an internal 3.3V power supply. This means the output signal cannot exceed 3.3V peak to peak and is unlikely to provide acceptable distortion levels above 2.8V peak to peak. This maximum output level (2.8V peak to peak) translates to approximately 1V **Root Mean Square (RMS)**.

The power available to a dynamic speaker in a headphone is $E^2/R$, so for 8 Ohm speakers, this means you could expect to have a maximum of 125 mW per audio channel. Unfortunately, the peak current required exceeds the capability of the PWM output, so unacceptable distortion may occur. However, if you use high-impedance headphones, for example, we use 32 Ohm Labtec C-105 headphones, the power output is reduced to 31 mW. In this case, no distortion occurs, but you will notice that the volume level is reduced.

# Understanding the ALSA configuration

Like so many things in the Linux, Debian, and Raspbian environments, the configuration of the sound capabilities is contained in files maintained by the OS. For **ALSA**, the configuration files are in the `/proc/asound` directory and can be viewed using File Manager or from the command prompt, as shown in the following screenshot:

In ALSA, the interfaces are associated with the concept of a card and, in larger computers, the audio adapter may be a physical card plugged into a backplane. In the command prompt view shown in the preceding screenshot, there are two cards shown. One is the internal bcm2825 (the chip number for the SOC in the Pi models prior to the 2-B) and the other is the Microsoft Webcam we attached to our system that has a microphone for audio capture.

There are several ALSA utilities that can be started at the command-line prompt:

* `alsamixer`: This utility provides controls for volume and can list card and device information

* `aplay`: This utility provides a means of playing PCM-encoded sound files and streams and lists playback devices

* `arecord`: This utility provides a means of capturing PCM audio and listing recording devices

A quick way to see all the audio devices on your Pi is to use the `alsamixer` utility. This utility provides a listing of the cards and devices. You also have the ability to set the play and record controls on the card. From a command prompt:

1. Type `alsamixer` to start the utility.
2. Select *F2* to view the contents of the `/proc/asound` directory.
3. Select *F6* to view the controls for a particular card.

You will need to know that supporting 5.1 and 7.1 channel output is a challenge for the BCM2825-based Pi due to the limited CPU resources. The new quad core BCM2836-based Model 2-B Pi can support more channels or multiple USB audio adapters. Refer to `https://sewelldirect.com/USB-SoundBox-71-and-51-Sound-Card_specs.asp` for more information. The following image shows the Sewell USB Sound adapter:

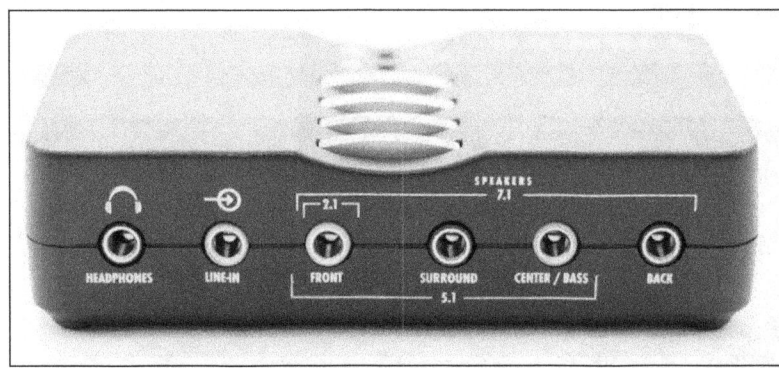

# Configuring the default device for ALSA

The ALSA configuration information will automatically treat card 0 as the default device. Unless you configure it otherwise, ALSA will remain pointed to either the Pi audio headphone port or to HDMI audio. The audio is configured when you install your instance of Raspbian and you connect your HDMI cable (if your display supports audio). If you plug in USB adapters in order to support better-quality audio or extended features, then you will need to create an `.asoundrc` file, which defines the default card to be used. This file is created in your home or user root directory; in our case, this is `/home` or `/home/pi`.

To create your own default setting in /home/pi, perform the following steps:

1. Open File Manager and go to **File | Create New.. | Blank File** to create an empty file called .asoundrc. Remember to turn on the **View Hidden files** option in File Manager or you won't be able to see it once created.

2. Right-click on .asoundrc and open the file in Leafpad.

3. Type the following text:

```
pcm.!default {
    type hw
    card 0
}
ctl.!default {
    type hw
    card 0
}
```

4. Save the file and exit.

> If you need further information on configuring ALSA, a good place to start is http://www.alsa-project.org/main/index.php/Asoundrc.

We have just completed a reset to the original default. When you plug in a new USB sound adapter, you can edit this file to make your new device the default. In our configuration, we changed the .asoundrc file to define card 3 as the default card. This allows my external USB adapter to be the default for all sound utilities rather than having to specify the device on the command line.

For example, to play a sound using aplay, you have to specify the device if you are not using the default card. If the default device is correctly set, then the command line could simply be aplay xxx.wav.

> To avoid confusion during the configuration process, we advise you to only configure your default card definition after you've installed the USB audio device and rebooted. You are then sure of consistent device ordering. For example, if you plug in a USB audio output device without turning off the computer, it is automatically allocated a new card number. In my example, the plug-in units were allocated cards 1, 2, and 3. If you now reboot the computer, the card number allocation may be different. In this case, the first, second and third USB devices in the USB tree (they are port sensitive) were now allocated as cards 0, 1, 2. The bcm2835 controller was allocated as card 3.

# Configuring the Raspberry Pi to support high-quality sound

Playing or capturing PCM audio is a very CPU-intensive and time-sensitive task. The data packets that define each block of acquired or moved data need to be handled with minimal latency. Otherwise, you may hear clicks, plops, or annoying gaps in the audio. You may even experience application hangs.

In *Chapter 3, Raspberry Pi and Cameras*, we discussed the ability to put the Pi into Turbo mode, which automatically raises and lowers the CPU clock frequency on demand. For the audio, we will need to turn this feature off to ensure that the Pi runs at a constant CPU frequency, thus ensuring that all the software timing is exact. We suggest that you fit a heat sink to the CPU. This will prevent the system software from cutting back the clock speed due to the excessive temperature rise.

If you turn on **Turbo** mode using the command `sudo raspi-config/overclock`, we recommend that you only use the **Medium** (900 MHz) setting, which is a more conservative setting for core overclocking frequencies.

For the quad processor Raspberry Pi model 2-B, the default clock speed for the 2/18/15 release of NOOBS was set at 600 MHz; for the earlier single processor models, by default, it is set to 700MHz. To enable the CPU to run at a higher speed, use the `raspi-config` command to set the overclock to 900 MHz (**Medium**).

The Turbo mode software governor is always set to `ondemand` when you turn the computer on and at each boot thereafter. You can see this setting by looking at the file `/sys/devices/system/cpu/cpu0/cpufreq/scaling_governor`. Using the on-demand setting, the CPU clock frequency is automatically increased if the CPU utilization is above 95 percent and a higher frequency is specified in the `/boot/config.txt` file (you can edit this or use the `raspi-config` command).

The `scaling_governor` setting can be set to a `conservative`, `ondemand`, `userspace`, `powersave`, or `performance` setting. The performance setting will increase the CPU frequency to the maximum you have set (900MHz) and keep it there.

For this exercise, we will set the `scaling_governor` setting to performance, which will always keep the frequency at 900 MHz unless the temperature of the SOC rises close to 85 degrees Celsius. To change `scaling_governor` to meet this requirement, we need to write a small Bash script to change the content of the file:

1. Using File Manager, create a new blank file, `set-perf`, in the `/home/pi` file location.

2. In the file properties, set it to executable.

3. Open the file in Leafpad and type the following script:

```
#!/bin/bash

#Set the cpu Turbo clock governor
case "$1" in
    +)
        echo "Setting clock scaling governor to performance"
        echo performance | sudo tee /sys/devices/system/cpu/cpu0/
cpufreq/scaling_governor          ;;
    -)
        echo "Setting clock scaling governor to ondemand"
        echo ondemand | sudo tee /sys/devices/system/cpu/cpu0/
cpufreq/scaling_governor

        ;;
    *)
        echo "usage ~./set-perf +|-"
        exit 1

        ;;
esac

exit 0
```

4. Save the file.

 Note that you can download the `set-perf` script file from `http://1drv.ms/1ysAxkl`.

You can now set the Turbo mode clock governor from the command line using +/- to indicate the state you want. For example, type `./set-perf` + to set the governor to `performance`.

To see the current CPU temperature and clock speed from the desktop, you can enable taskbar applets using the following steps:

1. Right-click on the taskbar and select **Add / Remove Panel items**.

2. From the **Panel Preferences** window, click on the **Panel Applets** tab. Add the **CPUFreq frontend** and **Temperature Monitor** panels.

3. Close the **Panel Preferences** window, and you will see the applets on the taskbar. Hover the mouse pointer over the applet icon to view it in greater detail.

The following screenshot shows the actions performed in the preceding steps:

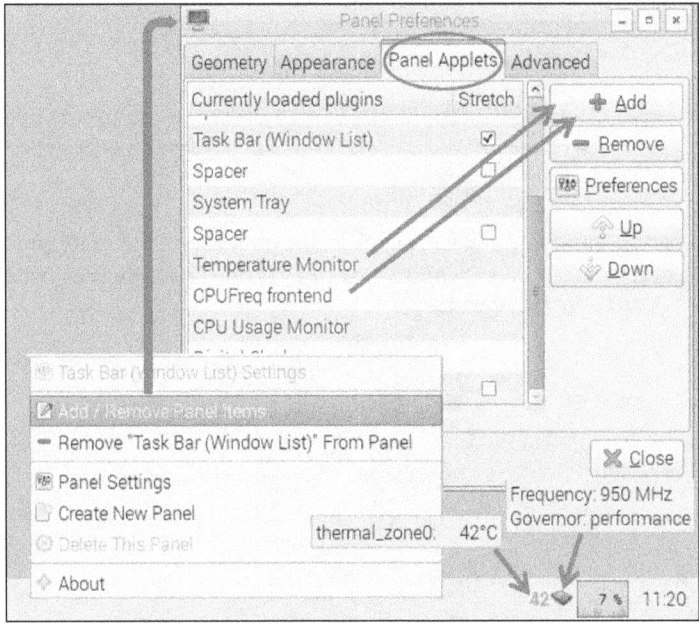

# Project 1 – Installing an advanced audio playback application

Although there are many applications and utilities that will allow playback of sound files and streams, we will introduce only one of them.

We will use the **VLC media player** (`http://www.videolan.org/vlc/index.html`). The VLC media player is available for a large range of operating systems and has a very rich feature set. After installation, you will need to make some immediate configuration changes. These changes ensure that VLC is better suited to the Pi environment and its resource limitations.

To install it on your Pi, complete the following steps:

1. Type `sudo apt-get -y install vlc` to install the software.
2. Once installed, the VLC media player is available from Menu under **Menu | Sound & Video | VLC Media Player**.
3. Start VLC and configure the following elements via the interface using **Tools | Preferences** and **Simple Settings**:
    1. In **Interface Settings**:
        ○ Clear **Integrate video in interface**
        ○ Clear **Show systray Icon**
        ○ Select **Allow only one instance**
    2. In Audio Settings
        ○ In the **Output Module** dropdown box, select `ALSA audio output`
        ○ In the **Device dropdown**, select `bcm2835`
        ○ Clear **Enable time stretching**
    3. In Video Settings
        ○ Clear **Enable Video**

4. Select **Save**. The configuration settings are now saved in `/home/pi/.config/vlc/vlcrc`.

5. Exit and then restart the VLC media player, and when the VLC media player starts up, select the **Playlist** icon or **View/Playlist** from the menu.

6. In the **Playlist** window, select **Internet**, and then **Icecast Radio Directory**, as shown in the screenshot following this information box:

 Please note that the radio station playlist will build, but be aware that this task can take up to several minutes as each Internet radio station is resolved and verified. While this process is underway, the CPU usage will be 100 percent. VLC will not be able to process this task and play a radio station simultaneously. Wait until the CPU usage drops before selecting a radio station to play.

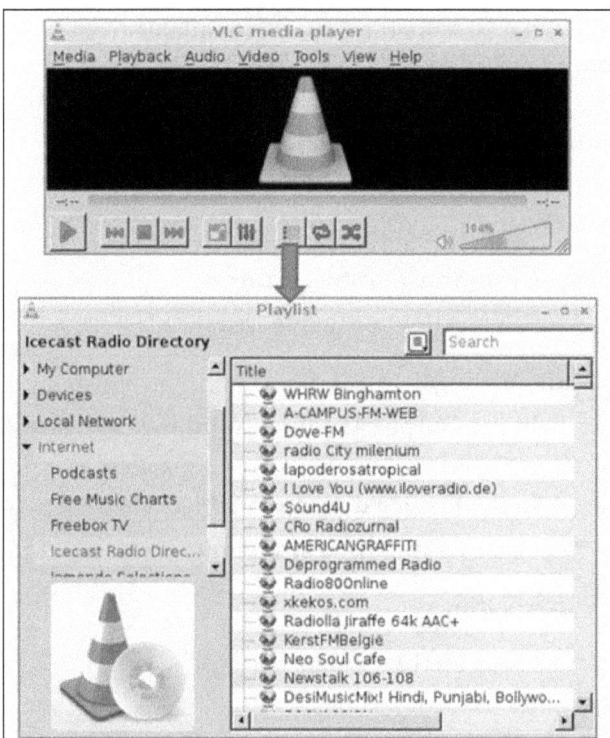

When the playlist is complete (CPU usage will now drop), you can double-click on any station in the list and it should play. It may take several seconds for the station to resolve and start playing.

Using the interface, you can see whether the station is playing when the **Pause** icon is present and the seek-time above it is incrementing. If the station you select does not play then, it may be that the bandwidth is insufficient and the connection timed out.

If the station is playing, and you cannot hear any sound from your output channels, select **Audio** from the menu. If the list is grayed out, then the audio is not playing. If the list is accessible, select **Audio | Audio Device**, and a list of output devices will be displayed. If you have everything configured correctly, the **bcm2835 ALSA** and **bcm2835 ALSA Default Audio Device** entries should be selected. From this selection, you can set the output device to be **bcm2835 ALSA** or select the appropriate channel from your plug-in USB audio adapter. As shown in the following image, our default device was my Logitech headphone. It is important that you do not select an interface capability that is not implemented on your audio adapter; if you do, it will not play audio.

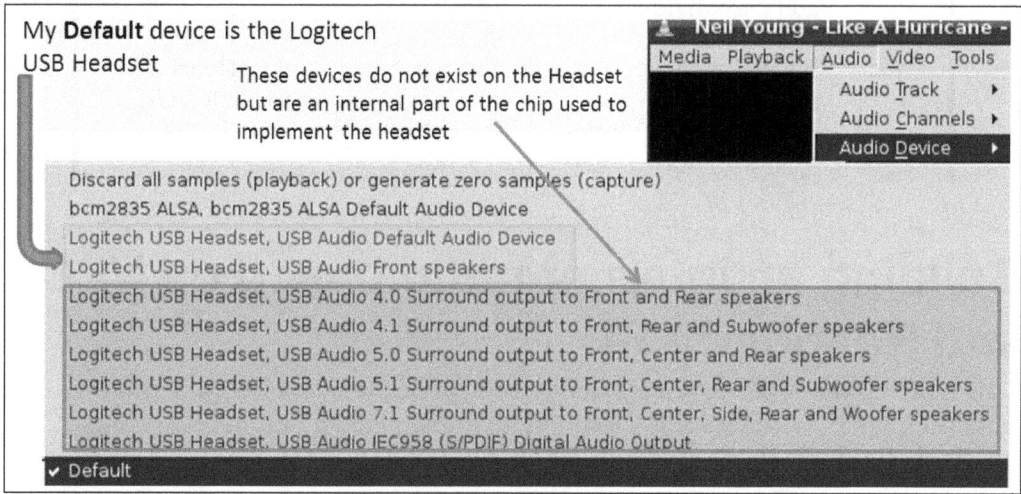

When a station is playing, you can examine **Tools | Media Information** to see the source URL used to access the stream and codec information about the stream.

From **Tools | Effects** and **Filters**, you can enable **Graphic Equalizer** and select bass and treble controls appropriate to your playback device. Any setting you select here is stored in the configuration file, so you only need to set them once.

You should now have the VLC media player running and be able to select any of the built-in **Icecast** directory of stations. Here are some website suggestions to explore and use to create your own playlist:

- `http://shoutcast.com`: This website has hundreds of worldwide Shoutcast streams sorted into genres. Simply open the web browser on your Pi, right-click on the download icon and copy the link address.

- `http://dir.xiph.org`: This website has hundreds of Icecast streams sorted into genres. In the browser, right-click on the M3U link and copy the link address.

- `http://bbcstreams.com`: This website has a range of BBC radio content. Right-click on the link and copy the link address.

- `http://listenlive.eu`: This website has a comprehensive list of content for countries in Europe. Right-click on the link and copy the link address.

To build your own playlist of favorite channels in the VLC media player, you can use **Media | Open Network Stream** and add the individual network URLs you copied above. This will add it to the playlist, but it will not be retained when you exit the VLC media player, so it's much better to build a playlist file with the URLs in it. The easiest form of playlist file to build is an M3U file. You can read the Videolan documentation at `https://wiki.videolan.org/M3U/`.

# Building an Internet radio based on VLC and Raspberry Pi

Now that we have VLC working as a desktop application, let's look at a project architecture that uses this audio capability to implement an Internet radio. First, let's define a basic feature set for our Internet radio:

- It should be able to play a broad range of Internet radio stations in stereo using the VLC media player.

- It should feature a radio **Play/Pause** capability.

- It should have a user interface to select a new radio station.

- It should provide a way to add new radio stations.

- It should load radio stations from a playlist file on application startup.
- Provides capability for remote interface. Since Python is portable across a broad range of platforms, you can run a remote interface on everything from Raspberry Pi, PC, and MAC with only minor modifications. The VLC process continues to run on the Pi.

The VLC process continues to run on the Pi. Our project architecture will look like this:

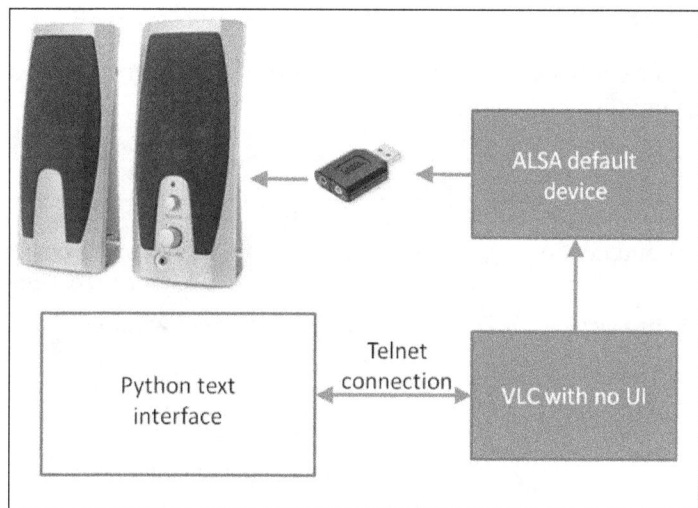

We'll discuss the implications of the architecture as we develop the interfaces to control the radio.

The project files for this chapter located at `http://1drv.ms/1ysAxkl` are as follows:

- `playlist`: This is a text file describing the content URLs/MRLs for the radio
- `parse.py`: This is a Python 3 example of parsing the playlist file
- `radio.py`: This is the Python 3 text-based radio with extensive debug messages that can be enabled to aid in understanding `logic.tktest.py`, which is the **TKinter** GUI interface, as a standalone example. You can start this with the IDLE3 shell/editor from a command prompt where you will see debug messages, or double-click and execute within File Manager, where you will then only have the GUI.
- `tkradio.py`: This is the full Tkinter Internet radio application.

# Project 2a – Running VLC in the background for the Internet radio

Now that we have the VLC media player working with a UI satisfactorily on the Pi, let's look at what it takes to automate its operation. The application has a complex UI, but we are about to turn all that complexity off. If you have the VLC media player running, close the interface, and we will bring up a manual remote control facility. The following is a simple introduction to the remote control that can be used to run the VLC media player without a GUI.

The following table shows the list and description of the commands that need to be run to get the manual remote working:

| Command | Description |
|---|---|
| Open a Terminal command prompt window and do the following: Type `cvlc -I telnet` | To start a **Telnet** server listening on port 4212 by default (this can be altered in the configuration file or GUI interface—search for LUA Telnet). |
| | Note that the command window shows information when VLC starts; don't worry about what appear to be errors, it is just that the VLC media player is choosing options to process the audio. As the VLC media player is sent remote control commands, the actions taken will be displayed in this command window. |
| Open a new Terminal command prompt window and do the following: Type `netcat localhost 4212` | The `netcat` application is an IP communications client; we can use it as a very simple Telnet client. As soon as it connects to the port for the VLC media player, the server sends a logon message and asks for a password. |
| | The default password is `admin`, but this can be altered in the VLC media player configuration files or from the GUI. |
| Type `admin` in response to the Password challenge. | You will get a welcome message and a ">" cursor; the VLC media player remote is now waiting for further commands. |
| Type `playlist`. | The server will respond with a printout of the playlist contents. There are no items in the playlist yet. |
| Start a web browser. | Go to `http://shoutcast.com` or another Internet radio channel provider. |

| Command | Description |
|---|---|
| From the Shoutcast interface select an appropriate radio station URL, right click on the download icon and copy the URL. | The URL will be in a format such as this: `http://yp.shoutcast.com/sbin/tunein-station.pls?id=216286` |
| In the Telnet session, type `add` and a space.<br><br>From the window menu, select **Edit** \| **Paste**, and the URL will be added to the command line. | The command line should now be similar to this: add `http://yp.shoutcast.com/sbin/tunein-station.pls?id=216286` When you type enter, the VLC media player will resolve the network location and start playing the station. The actions performed by the VLC media player will be shown in the first command window you opened; you will see that the VLC media player selected a decoding demuxer appropriate to the station's streaming format. |
| In the Telnet session, type `playlist`. | When the playlist is printed out this time, the entry you just made is shown. The VLC media player resolves the URL and the radio station should be playing. |

You can explore the Telnet interface for the VLC media player and get to know the commands that apply to just playing audio. Many of the commands apply to video and are of no concern to this project. To get a complete list of commands, simply type "help" at the Telnet session prompt. In particular, you can try the following commands from the Telnet session: `Quit`, `Add`, `Start`, `Stop`, `Clear`, `Status`, `stats`, `title`, `Info`, `Volume`, `Volup`, and `Voldown`.

The Telnet interface will work from any computer that can connect to your Pi. While we specified localhost as the address, this is equivalent to 127.0.0.1, which is simply the local loopback interface. You could easily access the VLC media player Telnet server from any computer using its current IP address. For example, my wired Pi Ethernet IP address is `192.168.3.77:4212`.

 You have to specify the IP address if you want to access the VLC media player instance remotely via Telnet. Specifying only localhost during configuration prevents the instance from responding to external Telnet requests.

# Starting VLC automatically at reboot

Since our plan is to automate the operation of the VLC media player, now is a great time to ensure that the VLC media player starts as a **daemon** every time we turn on the Pi. We've been through this process before, so it should be easy. We'll improve our methodology to ensure simplified future starts of the reboot process.

During development, you may want to add or delete multiple applications to the `@reboot` capability of **crontab**. One flexible way for a developer is to add a single pointer to a shell script in the crontab. For example, for our current development, we performed the following steps:

1.  Run `crontab -e` and type a single line `@reboot /home/pi/.atreboot` to the crontab.

2.  Create a file called `.atreboot` in your `/home/pi` folder. You need to remember that this is a hidden file.

3.  Edit `.atreboot` to contain the list of actions you want performed in the boot process.

4.  Set the executable property on the file.

The following is a screenshot of my `.atreboot`:

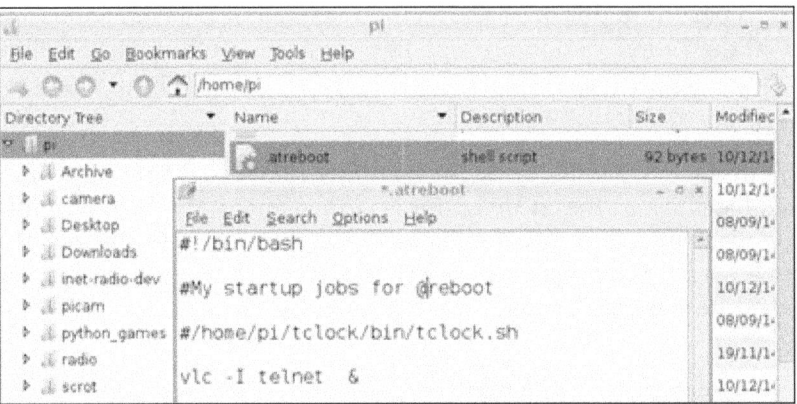

Before we start cutting code for the interface, you need to have the VLC media player running with the Telnet interface enabled. If the VLC media player is not yet running, there are several ways you can do this:

*   Reboot your Pi if you have just set up for the VLC media player to be started at reboot.

*   Start the VLC media player from a Terminal command prompt so that it provides a view of the VLC media player actions being performed.

Execute `/home/pi/.atreboot` from a Terminal command prompt or file manager. Let's get started and set up the directories needed for the project:

- Create a directory called `/home/pi/radio`
- Create a directory called `/home/pi/radio/bin`

You can download project files for this chapter at `http://1drv.ms/1ysAxkl`.

# Project 2b – Designing a playlist file for the Internet radio

Let's get started and set up a playlist file for the project:

1. Create a blank file in `/home/pi/radio` called `playlist`

2. Edit playlist in Leafpad and add station information as two comma-separated elements, as shown in the following list:

   ◦ The entries consist of `<station-description>`, `<URL/MRL>` pairs on the same line. Neither text file can contain `","` as it is used as a delimiter between fields. Note that some Internet radio station URLs may be very long (80 characters or more).

   ◦ A good site to start with is `http://shoutcast.com`, where you can get some short station URLs to experiment with.

The following screenshot shows a playlist that I created; you can download this playlist from `http://1drv.ms/1ysAxkl`:

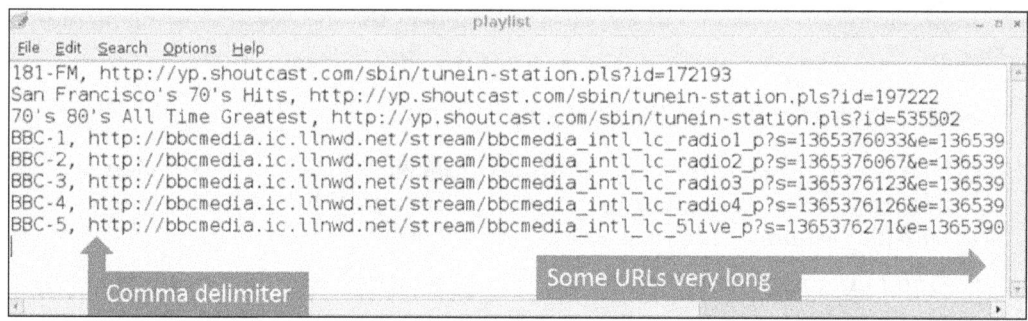

All of the URLs used here are `http://` but the VLC media player is able to resolve and access many types of **Media Resource Locator (MRL)**, such as the `file://` MRLs The Internet radio is able to play any valid sound stream MRLs, and you might like to try the following if you have media stored, although some code modification is required:

```
file:///path/file              #Play media file or content in
directory
ftp://host[:port]/file         #FTP URL
udp://[[<source address>]@[<bind address>][:<bind port>]]
                               #UDP stream sent by a streaming
server
```

## Chapter 4 supplemental materials

As a learning exercise, there is additional material in the `Chapter 4` folder download that shows the implementation of file parsing and a Python text mode interface for the radio. Please read and complete this work before proceeding to understand the progression of the design from the text mode to the GUI.

# Project 2c – Parsing the playlist file for the Internet radio

Now that we have the playlist file defined and have added some entries, you need to be able to read the file and build the internal data structures that will be used to hold station data in the Internet radio. You can download the `parse.py` file and the `Chapter 4` supplemental materials document from `http://1drv.ms/1ysAxkl`. The methodology for testing `parse.py` is available in the `Chapter 4` supplemental materials.

The **parse.py** program will do the following actions:

- Open and read the Internet station streams we want from a file called `/home/radio/playlist`Prints out of a numerical list of the stations in the playlist file

- Print out the station list `python list[]`, which is used later to allow access to the entries.

# Project 2d – Implementing a Python text interface to VLC

The methodology for testing the radio.py file is available in the Chapter 4 supplemental materials folder. It is a simple text interface with the following features:

- It reads the Internet station streams we want from a file called /home/radio/playlist

- It shows the first item in the playlist is the default item, and it will play as soon as the application loads

- It prints out a list of the stations in the playlist file

- It allows you to enter a station number to start playing any station

- It implements a simple retry mechanism if stations don't start to play within 2 seconds

- It allows you to enter '0' to exit the program

# Project 3 – Implementing a TKinter GUI for the Internet radio

TKinter is a standard GUI framework for Python and extends the command-line driven Python interface to a window-based interface. Window-based interfaces are typically user event driven, and this significantly reduces the amount of programming required to design a GUI. In the case of a TKinter/Python application, the task is split into roughly the following components:

- **UI definition and initialization code**: This is typically a collection of frames, buttons, textboxes, dialogs, canvases, and so on, which are positioned in a TK window.

- **Definition and initialization of event handlers**: Since the UI responds directly to the user input (mouse/touch or keyboard actions), the event handlers perform all the actions required by the event. For example, pressing a button on the UI could perform all the actions required if the event handler had code for it. In many cases, however, there may be messages transferred to other tasks (threads) that might also complete the actions. Optional parallel tasks perform background processing not associated with the UI user input.

- **Starting the window event loop**: This boils down to a single statement that starts the task responsible for monitoring the events for the UI.

The elements required for our Internet radio are:

- A base window to hold all components
- Labels to identify UI functions
- Buttons to capture action directives
- A spinbox that holds the station list

TKinter uses a very simple column-and-row placement paradigm for laying out interface elements within the UI and for default sizing. The following image (we won't discuss the code for it) shows a calculator interface where you can easily see the rows and columns that were used. TKinter automatically packs the elements you place within the window and, unless you specify otherwise, it will make the columns and rows the same size. The results textbox at the top of this calculator was defined as spanning four columns using a configuration option called `rowspan`.

# Running tktest.py

Before we can begin this next exercise, you will need to download the `tktest.py` program from `http://1drv.ms/1ysAxkl` and place it in the `/home/pi/radio/bin` folder. As you review the script, take note of the comments embedded in the code (preceded by "#"); their primary purpose is to help describe the code functionality. User input is limited to the up/down scroll buttons, and the start/stop buttons. You will also see that there is output from the console that describes the interface activity when you press a button; this can be turned off by setting a variable called debug to `False`. Additionally, the radio and clock functionality is contained within the window event handler functions defined.

# Creating a clock in the radio UI

Let's look at one particular function in the code used to create the interface clock. To create the clock, `update_clock()` calls the function that builds a time string and stores it in a TKinter variable called `vtime`. These special TKinter variables can be bound to the interface elements and you will see that, in the `timeLabel` definition, there is a configuration for `textvariable=vtime`. This binds the variable to the label, and any time `vtime` is updated, the label text changes without requiring any programmatic actions.

To get the clock to 'tick' regularly, the `update_clock()` function registers a callback with the root container to call itself after 500 ms. The root container can maintain many callback timers such as this in a queue, and it's an easy way to get functions to repeat regularly and immediately update the interface elements. Here's how this is done:

```
def update_clock():
    vtime.set( time.strftime(" %a %B %d  %l:%M:%S %p "))
    root.after(500, update_clock)

timeLabel= Label(primaryFrame, textvariable=vtime,
          font=("Helvetica", 22),
          fg="white", bg="black" ).grid(row=13, column=0,
                                  padx=10, pady=10)
```

Note in the preceding code fragments that `vtime` is the TKinter variable that is bound to the `timelabel` clock display as `textvariable=vtime`. Every 500 ms, the `update_clock()` function is called and `vtime.set` updates the time string.

The following image shows you what the window will look like when rendered and how the major program elements relate to the interface; you will notice that the clock keeps time without any programming effort:

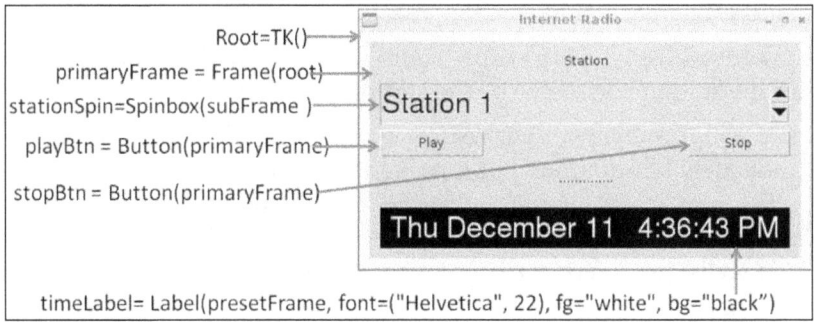

You should be able to relate the aforementioned code to the rendered screen when you run the program. You can reference the documentation for TKinter at `https://docs.python.org/3.2/library/tk.html` to learn the meaning and syntax of the functions used. One particularly helpful documentation site is `http://www.tutorialspoint.com/python/python_gui_programming.htm`. Here, you will find excellent coverage of the difference between the `pack()` and `grid()` placement managers. Our next task is to merge the text-based Python code with the TKinter GUI code to achieve our final project. The code is also organized to be read serially from top to bottom to make it easier for you to read through.

# Running tkradio.py

Download the `tkradio.py` program and place it in the `/home/pi/radio/bin` folder.

This code is the complete implementation of the radio using Python 3/TKinter with a GUI user interface. The VLC media player application should already be running if you followed through the earlier tasks and supplemental materials content. You can check with Task Manager and also log in to it via Telnet to check whether VLC is functioning. When you download the code, you will notice that it is laid out as a group of defined functions very similar to the Python 3 text mode implementation. These functions implement the radio logic as described in the following steps:

1. `def ParsePlaylist(filename):` This opens the playlist file, prints a count number and station description, and finally returns the information to create the station array list.

2. `def CreateSession( host, port, timeout):` This connects to the VLC Telnet server and uses a `try:`/`except:` block to capture timeouts or connection failures. One tricky note here is that the Telnet protocol uses a strict ASCII character stream, so the `.encode` function converts the internal default UTF-8 format to ASCII.

3. `def AddStationtoPlaylist( stationnum):` This uses the add command with the station URL to write the station URL to the VLC playlist.

4. `def ClearPlaylist():` The reason for using this function may not immediately be apparent, but it prevents the number of entries in the VLC playlist from accumulating. It uses the clear command to reset the VLC playlist. You might notice, however, that the numerical identifiers for the VLC playlist just keep incrementing as you clear and add to `playlist.def`.

5. `stopradio()`: This uses the stop command to stop audio playing.

6. `def PlayRadio()`: This provides the initialization logic and a while loop to interface with the user.

There are two `TKinter` variables used, one to update the time display and the other to keep track of the scroll box count, which is called the spin count. Within the `TKinter` code block, there are functions defined to handle each of the interface buttons and the Spinbox up and down controls.

The TKinter interface elements and frame are used to improve the overall design of the radio, and the following three commands kick it off:

* `playradio()`: This function starts the process of parsing the playlist and establishing Telnet communication with the VLC application

* `update_clock`: This function starts updating the clock

* `root.mainloop()`: This function starts the TK window message loop task

So, there we have it—a fully functional GUI-based Internet radio, with a clock, that can support hundreds of entries in the playlist if you need it to. Based on this design, you might like to consider extending the code and interface to include functions such as:

* Adding a set of alarm functions for the clock

* Using more of VLC's command set, such as `pause`, `voldown`, `volup`, and `vol x`

* Playing media libraries from directories on USB keys or network locations (and using the VLC random command to randomize the playlist)

* Changing the `HOST` string to the Raspberry Pi IP address in the LUA Telnet configuration instead of using localhost so that you can run the interface remotely on another Pi (or even a PC or Mac)

# Recording sound files on the Pi

Previously, we wanted to set up a single default identifier for sound to ease the challenge of selecting speaker devices. However, when it comes to acquiring sound from microphones, we might need some more flexibility to individually address multiple microphones on our system. We altered our configuration a little to show some of the options you might want to explore. We have the Sewell USB Audio adapter connected to the USB hub that has multiple microphone inputs (stereo and mono) and a Line input. This device also supports up to a 7.1 sound although we are only using 2.1 here.

Also connected to the USB hub is the Microsoft Lifecam Studio, which has a really terrific stereo, high-gain, noise-cancelling microphone. This is a great microphone for voice command systems due to the good quality of audio with little echo or reverberation problems.

Using the `lsusb` and `alsamixer` commands in the Terminal, we can quickly look at connected devices with their capabilities and associated information:

```
pi@raspberrypi: ~                                              _ □ ✕

File  Edit  Tabs  Help
pi@raspberrypi ~ $ lsusb
Bus 001 Device 002: ID 0424:9514 Standard Microsystems Corp.
Bus 001 Device 001: ID 1d6b:0002 Linux Foundation 2.0 root hub
Bus 001 Device 008: ID 413c:3012 Dell Computer Corp. Optical Wheel Mouse
Bus 001 Device 013: ID 045e:0772 Microsoft Corp. LifeCam Studio
Bus 001 Device 012: ID 0d8c:0102 C-Media Electronics, Inc. CM106 Like Sound Devi
ce
Bus 001 Device 003: ID 0424:ec00 Standard Microsystems Corp.
Bus 001 Device 004: ID 0bda:8176 Realtek Semiconductor Corp. RTL8188CUS 802.11n
WLAN Adapter
Bus 001 Device 005: ID 1a40:0101 Terminus Technology Inc. 4-Port HUB
Bus 001 Device 006: ID 413c:2105 Dell Computer Corp. Model L100 Keyboard
Bus 001 Device 007: ID 1a40:0101 Terminus Technology Inc. 4-Port HUB
pi@raspberrypi ~ $ █
```

In the preceding `lsusb` listing, you can see that Microsoft Lifecam is device `013` and the Sewell USB Audio adapter is the C-Media Electronics device `012`. Note that they have particular USB device IDs because we did not reboot but simply plugged them in. If we rebooted the Pi, the numbers would change, but the USB ports would remain the same (`lsusb -t`).

If you make selections in the `alsamixer` interface, they are saved on shutdown and automatically loaded again when you start the Pi. You can easily set up all of the playback and capture levels and capture configuration and have it remain constant.

As part of the ALSA utilities, there is the `aplay` utility that plays sound files and the `arecord` utility that captures sound files.

These command-line utilities can be a little tricky to get going, so here's a procedure that will help:

1. With File Manager, create a directory named `/home/pi/recorder` by navigating to **File | Create New | Folder**.

2. Open the `recorder` directory.

3. Navigate to **Tools | Open Current Folder in Terminal** to open a Terminal session window.

4. In the terminal session window, enter `arecord -L   | grep 'sysdefault'`.

5. In the terminal session window, enter `aplay -L   | grep 'sysdefault'`.

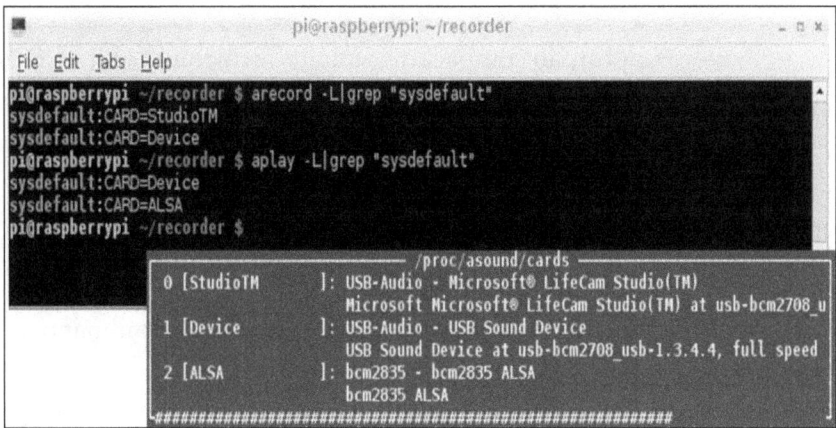

You can see in the preceding screenshot that Microsoft Lifecam only appears in the `arecord` output along with the Sewell USB Audio adapter (name of `Device` is a little confusing). In the `aplay` output, only devices that support sound output are shown, and ALSA is the name used for the Pi `bcm2835` sound output.

We can use these names to directly address sound output or sound acquisition to the specific device we want to use.

To record a sound file and then play it back, do the following:

1. Open a terminal session window with `/home/pi/recorder` as the working folder.

2. Using the name of your capture device, enter your variation of `arecord -D sysdefault:StudioTM -c 2 -f cd -V stereo -d 30 test.wav`.

   For the preceding command, the options mean the following:

   ○ `-D sysdefault:StudioTM`: Use a friendly name to identify the required device. We don't need to specify USB endpoints because the utility knows how to resolve the capture device,

   ○ `-c 2`: Capture two channels.

   ○ `-f cd`: Capture in compact disc quality, which is 16 bit 44.1Khz.

   ○ `-V`: Show the text-based stereo VU meter.

   ○ `-d 30`: Capture for 30 seconds.

   ○ `Test.wav`: This is the file to capture the encoded audio to. This could be a full pathname.

   You can use `arecord -h` to see the help.

The following screenshot shows you the ouput to the preceding command
I explained:

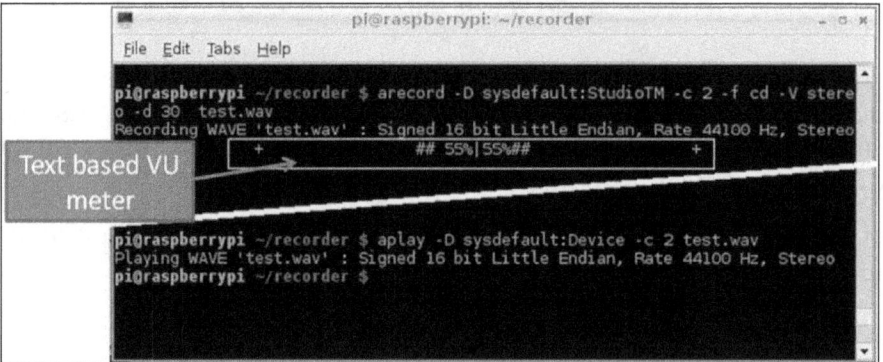

You will notice that the utilities take several seconds to start acquisition or playback. In the preceding output image, note that we captured from the Microsoft Lifecam stereo microphone and played the sound back through the Sewell USB Audio adapter.

Although the `arecord` utility only consumes about 7 percent of the CPU while recording CD-quality sound, it has demanding latency issues. If you start an application that requires a lot of CPU (for example, starting the browser), you will see dropped buffers, which result in audible defects in the capture.

Now that we've completed the Internet radio project, you are also able to capture good quality sound files using the ALSA utilities. This gives you a good technical grounding on many of the issues surrounding playback and capture of audio. We hope that it has given you some great design ideas for future projects.

To summarize some of the important points you need to remember when designing good quality audio support using the Pi:

- Always make sure that the Pi is not overloaded and that the CPU is at a fixed frequency and not using the `ondemand` governor setting, which will raise and lower the clock speed dynamically. If you are using resource intensive applications such as VLC, make sure you understand any configuration issues when using it on the Pi. VLC is resource hungry and your first few configuration tasks in this chapter were about ensuring it would run successfully on the Pi.

- Configuring defaults for ALSA will significantly reduce configuration issues with your sound I/O devices. Remember that, while Raspbian provides immense flexibility with ad hoc addition and removal of USB devices, you need to ensure that you have a consistent reboot setup so that your devices are where you expect them to be. Many USB audio adapters are based on the same silicon chips. These chips sometimes have capabilities far beyond those exposed by the device. For example, Microsoft Lifecam uses a chip that supports 7.1 speakers, microphones, and SP/Diff, but it only exposes the stereo microphones. Don't get confused by what features are shown in an application such as VLC.

# Summary

Now that we've completed the fourth chapter, let's review some of the main tasks you learned to do:

- You configured the Raspberry Pi to support the internal audio output device and add-on USB audio adapters
- You installed and configured USB sound devices under ALSA
- You installed and configured VLC to play Internet-based "radio" streams
- You created a Python text interface to automate VLC
- You created and modified a fully-featured TKinter interface to implement a stereo Internet radio with a clock
- You acquired audio from a microphone connected to the USB audio adapter

In the next chapter, you will start to exercise some of the Raspberry Pi input and output ports to drive LEDs and displays and sense physical switches.

# 5
# Port Input and Output on the Raspberry Pi

Digital input and output (I/O) is at the point where computer programming touches the real world. The Raspberry Pi has a rich I/O structure that includes 3.3 Volts, input and output interface ports, **Serial Peripheral Interface (SPI)**, and **Inter-Integrated Circuit (I2C)**. Using this I/O structure, you will drive LEDs as output indicators and then use the **Tkinter** interface to sense switches as input.

After completing this chapter, you will be able to:

- Understand the Raspberry Pi digital I/O port configuration
- Drive LEDs and sense actuation of switches
- Add a switch interface to the Internet radio project

## Understanding Raspberry Pi digital input and output ports

The Broadcom SOC (BCM2835 and BCM2836 in the Raspberry Pi Model 2-B) used to implement the Raspberry Pi is a CMOS device, and the I/O ports are driven by 3.3V logic gates. When connecting direct internal functionality such as digital I/O ports to the outside world or exposing them to the outside world via external wiring, there are risks involved. A single digital port might be programmatically configured to be an input or an output, and with a pull-up or pull-down termination. The ports are directly connected to the Pi SOC computer chip. These ports are static and load sensitive; the wrong load types and high voltages could potentially damage the CPU.

The following image shows a typical I/O port configuration for the digital I/O ports on this type of SOC. While there is an output-enable to turn on the port driver, the input buffer can always detect the logic level of the GPIO pin. Note that, in this typical implementation, there are clamping diodes across the input pin, so a connection to the 5V external logic could permanently damage the SOC.

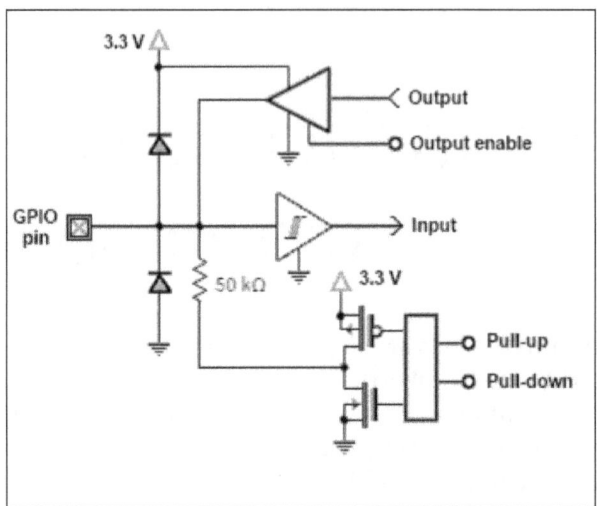

# Using breakout boards with the Raspberry Pi

The Raspberry Pi B+ has a 40-pin header that presents signals that can be taken off the motherboard for experimentation. You can use shields designed for the Raspberry Pi to implement physical I/O, but they are typically designed with specific functions on the board. A more experimental approach is to use breadboards that have an array of small sockets that allow you to push components and wires into the connection points. Breadboards are reusable, and you won't need to solder wires and components.

In the following image, my Raspberry Pi B+ is shown connected to a **CanaKit** GPIO breakout board inserted in a small solderless breadboard. The I/O pin layout shown is for the Raspberry Pi A+, B+, and Model 2-B only.

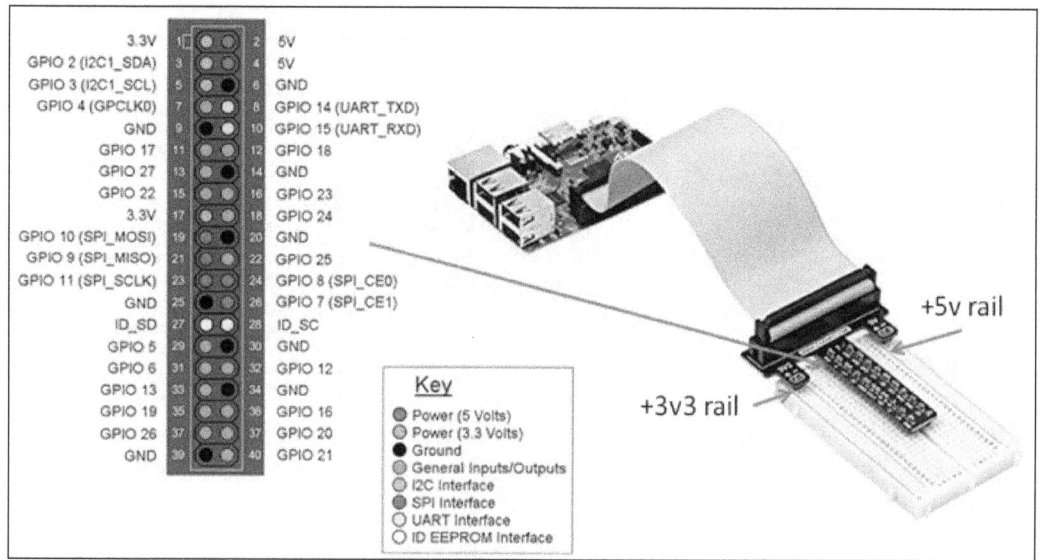

There are several suppliers of breakout adapters and breadboards, but the two boards that we recommend are:

- Canakit B+ GPIO Breakout has extra connections, which bring the 5V and 3.3V supplies to the outer rails on the breadboard. Visit `http://www.canakit.com/raspberry-pi-cobbler-gpio-breakout.html` for more details on the Canakit B+ GPIO breakout board.

- Adafruit accessories for the Raspberry Pi are very flexible. They have **T-Cobbler Plus GPIO Breakout** and inline **Cobbler GPIO Breakout**, and for those making more permanent interfaces, they have **Perma-Proto HAT** for the Raspberry Pi A+/B+ and Model 2-B. Visit `http://www.adafruit.com/categories/163` for more information on the T-Cobbler GPIO breakout board.

To make sure you understand the layout of the breadboard, the following is an image of the breadboard with the rows that the Pi signals will be on and a schematic of internal tracks and power busses:

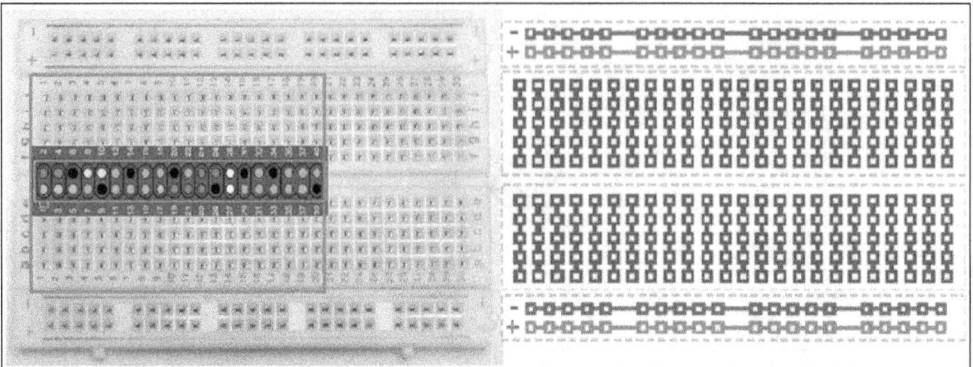

Note that, when you connect the cable to the Raspberry Pi, you have to be careful that you don't use too much force. Make sure that it is correctly aligned and be careful not to bend the motherboard.

Once you are all hooked up to the Pi, we can work through *Hello World* for LEDs. Then we will make an LED turn on and off using various programs.

# Driving LEDs as output indicators

LED indicators can take many forms, from a single LED indicator through to complex LED X-Y arrays and digit displays. If you have multiple indicator LEDs, it is preferable to include an LED driver and even better to offload this to an I2C controller, which we will explain in *Chapter 6, Driving I2CPeripherals on the Raspberry Pi*. If you have just a few LEDs to drive and are short of output pins for each LED, you will want to read up on **Charlieplexing** as a way of reducing the port count required (http://en.wikipedia.org/wiki/Charlieplexing).

For our demo, we will use a single LED attached to a single GPIO port. We will attach it to the GPIO 26 port with a series resistor to limit the current through the device. This is what your breadboard should look like, along with the schematic:

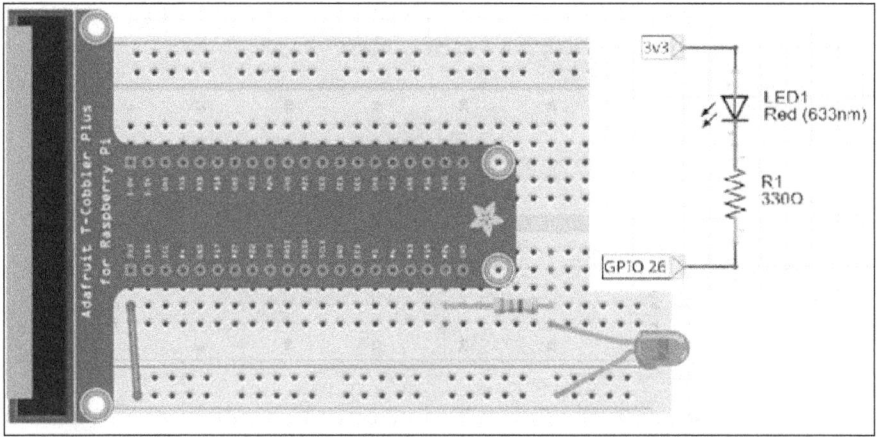

When the GPIO pin number 26 is high, the LED is off, and when it is low, a current of approximately 4 mA flows from the 3.3V supply through the LED and into the GPIO pin to the ground. Once you have an LED connected, as shown in the preceding image, we can develop some software to drive it.

# Python LED demo

Writing software to control digital I/O ports using RPi.GPIO requires root privileges. The required privileges might be acquired by membership of a group or from raising the privilege level of your application by using the sudo command. If the account you are logged in with is allowed to use sudo, as with pi as user, then using it from the command line is easy. We've taken the simple approach here of raising the application privilege level using sudo assuming always that you are logged in as the user pi.

We will start our demo with a simple Python program:

1. Open File Manager and create a new directory called gpio at /home/pi/.

2. In the /home/pi/gpio directory, create a new blank file called LED.py.

3. In file permissions, mark it as executable.

4. Open a Terminal session and, at the command prompt, type sudo idle3.

5. In the Python shell, use **File** | **Open** to start an editor window with /home/pi/gpio/LED.py as the current file.

6. Type the following code in **Editor Window** or download the LED.py file from the Chapter 5 folder at http://1drv.ms/1ysAxkl:

```
#!/usr/bin/python3

import RPi.GPIO as GPIO
from time import sleep

GPIO.setmode(GPIO.BCM)
GPIO.setup(26, GPIO.OUT, pull_up_down=GPIO.PUD_UP,
initial=1)

try:
    while True :                 #endless loop
        print(" Select 1=LED ON, 2=LED OFF, 3=21 second
timed loop then exit")
        inkey=input("?: ")
        if inkey == "1" :
            print("on")
            GPIO.output(26, 0)
        elif inkey == "2":
            print("off")
            GPIO.output(26, 1)
        elif inkey == "3":
            print("break")
            break              #break out of while loop

    count=0
    while (count < 400):     # 400 * 50mS -- approx 20
seconds
        GPIO.output(26, 0)
        sleep(0.025)
        GPIO.output(26, 1)
        sleep(0.025)
        count +=1
except KeyboardInterrupt:
        print("Keyboard break")

GPIO.cleanup()
exit()
```

Here is a list of code elements that you need to pay particular attention to:

- The importing of RPi.GPIO and a single function (sleep) from time.

- The GPIO.setmode configures the identifiers for either BOARD or BCM. We use BCM to indicate the Broadcom identifiers shown on the digital I/O pins, for example, GPIO 26.

- GPIO.setup defines the port, direction, termination, and initial state of the pin.

- GPIO.output defines the port and the value (0, 1) to be output.

- GPIO.cleanup sets any port that has been programmed away from default, back to the default settings. This command does not reset all ports and, with program faults, you might get a warning error. This can safely be ignored, but you can read the documentation for configurations that stop this type of error.

> Find the full documentation at
> http://sourceforge.net/projects/raspberry-gpio-python.

The initial code provides a pre-configuration, and the function code in the try:/except: block does the main work of controlling the LED. Entering 1 or 2 at the user input prompt turns the LED on or off by setting the port low or high. Entering *Ctrl + C* on the keyboard will cause an exception and will then exit from the program.

Entering 3 on the keyboard at the user prompt will *break* out of the user input, while loop and enters a block of code where the on and off time is defined by two *sleep* statements. This is not a very practical way to control indicators in a project, but it does demonstrate the following points:

- The sleep statements pause all program execution until they time out. If you wanted the LED to flash, you could adjust it two times to get an acceptable flash rate for an indicator. However, you would be stuck in your program loop until it stops flashing unless you include all your code in the while loop.

- If you want to modulate the brightness of an LED, you could adjust the times again, but the times will become very low (just a few milliseconds each), and the program will utilize more resources just doing the timer function.

> Using inline timers in code is not a very practical way to provide a user interface and is very difficult to manage.

# TKinter LED demo

Now, let's explore a window-based interface with more examples of how to drive LEDs.

The code is divided into sections and includes a summary of the functionality for the major blocks but not all of the code. Review the code and the summaries following the image before you download the code from `http://1drv.ms/1ysAxkl`

In order for you to have a mental model of the LED demo as you read through the code, here is the TKinter interface (GPIO test) when rendered:

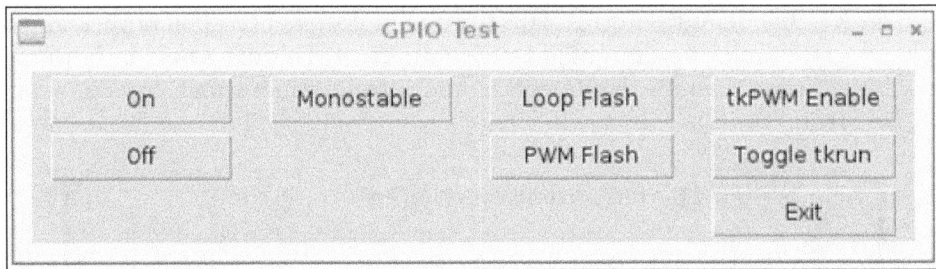

# Block 1 – initialization

This block loads the required libraries, does initial setup, and defines the TKinter window. It is possible to set the window size here but, in this code, I simply allow the window size to be defined by the elements it contains:

```
#!/usr/bin/python3

from tkinter import *
from time import sleep
import RPi.GPIO as GPIO

GPIO.setmode(GPIO.BCM)
GPIO.setup(26, GPIO.OUT, pull_up_down=GPIO.PUD_UP, initial=1)

#Python variable
debug=True
tkrun=0
```

```
tkenable=0
out=0

#Define the TKinter window
root = Tk() #Makes the window
root.wm_title("GPIO Test") # Window title
root.config(background = "#FFFFF0")
```

You will notice that this block is nearly identical to the Python code in LED.py, with the addition of some Python global variables being initialized and the definition of the TKinter window.

# Block 2 – on/off buttons

This is the code to handle switch activity directly from the TKinter button elements:

```
#Event handlers for interface elements
def onbtnPress():
    if ( debug ): print ("On Button Pressed")
    GPIO.output(26, 0)

def offbtnPress():
    if ( debug ): print ("Off Button Pressed")
    GPIO.output(26, 1)

#Button definitions
onBtn = Button(primaryFrame, text="On", command=onbtnPress,
width=10)
onBtn.grid(row=1, column=0, padx=10, pady=2)

offBtn = Button(primaryFrame, text="Off", command=offbtnPress,
width=10)
offBtn.grid(row=2, column=0, padx=10, pady=2)
```

This block shows two buttons that turn the LED on/off. The action takes place in the functions called onbtnPress() and offbtnPress(), which use the GPIO.output() function to set the port value.

# Block 3 – monostable function

This code implements a monostable function for a single LED; it also defines the TKinter buttons:

```
def monobtnPress():
    if ( debug ): print("Mono Flash button pressed ")
    GPIO.output(26, 0)                #Turn LED on
    root.after(100, tkmono)           #start a tk timer

def tkmono():
    GPIO.output(26, 1)                #turn LED off

monoBtn = Button(primaryFrame, text="Monostable",
command=monobtnPress, width=10)
monoBtn.grid(row=3, column=0, padx=10, pady=2)
```

This block has a handler for the **Monostable** button, which turns the LED on, and then registers a `tk` timer (`root.after`) callback to `tkmono()`. The timer is asynchronous and will call `tkmono` soon after the 100 ms expires. Timers such as this are not meant to be very accurate, but it is always better than a millisecond or so. The nice thing about doing LED control this way is that your code is free to go on (and the TKinter interface is responsive) to other tasks. This same technique can be used to control many LEDs as the timers are just queued.

# Block 4 – loop flash

This block uses sleep timers, which are not the best way to implement LED control:

```
def loopbtnPress():
    if ( debug ): print("Loop Flash button pressed ")
    count=0
    out=0
    while (count < 100):
        GPIO.output(26, out)
        sleep(0.05)
        out=(out+1)%2
        count +=1
    GPIO.output(26, 1)

loopBtn = Button(primaryFrame, text="Loop Flash",
command=loopbtnPress, width=10)
loopBtn.grid(row=4, column=0, padx=10, pady=2)
```

You will notice that this block is very similar to the loop block in the LED.py file. This version only uses one sleep timer but is essentially the same in operation. Note that when you use the interface, the **Loop Flash** button stays depressed and the interface is nonresponsive for the length of the count. This type of code implementation is not the best way to provide a good user experience.

# Block 5 – PWM flash

This block of code uses the library PWM function but, since it has to also use sleep timers, it is not an ideal solution:

```
def pwmbtnPress():
    if ( debug ): print("PWM button pressed ")
    mypwm=GPIO.PWM(26,10)
    mypwm.start(50)
    sleep(5.0)
    mypwm.stop()
    sleep(0.02)
    GPIO.output(26, 1)

pwmBtn = Button(primaryFrame, text="PWM Flash",
command=pwmbtnPress, width=10)
pwmBtn.grid(row=5, column=0, padx=10, pady=2)
```

This block starts to show some of the extra functionality in the RPi.GPIO library. The GPIO.PWM constructor allows the creation of a fixed-frequency, programmable-duty-cycle pulse width modulator. The duty cycle can be changed programmatically using .ChangeDutyCycle() once you have created the PWM object. In this simple exercise, where we are simply flashing the LED, it's unfortunately hindered by the use of sleep timers again, but it is possible to create a TK timer to make it more flexible. We would not recommend the PWM for the control of servos since the duty-cycle errors tend to be higher than the deadzone setting for most servos. We will discuss this in more depth when we discuss I2C peripherals in *Chapter 6, Driving I2C Peripherals on the Raspberry Pi.*

# Block 6 – TKPWM flash and toggle tkrun

This is the best of the solutions for driving LEDs within an interface; it uses TKinter timers to control the LED ON-times:

```python
def tkpwm():
        global out
        global tkrun
        global tkenable
        if (tkenable == 1):
            if (tkrun == 1):
                GPIO.output(26, out)
                out=((out + 1) %2)
            else:
                GPIO.output(26, 1)
        root.after(50, tkpwm)


def tkbtnPress():
    global tkrun
    global tkenable
    if ( debug ): print("tkPWM button pressed ")
    if (tkBtn["text"] == "tkPWM Enable" ):
        tkBtn["text"]="tkPWM Disable"
        tkenable=1
    else:
        tkBtn["text"]="tkPWM Enable"
        tkenable=0


def tglbtnPress():
    global tkrun
    if ( debug ): print("Toggle tkrun button pressed ")
    tkrun=((tkrun+1) % 2)
tkBtn = Button(primaryFrame, text="tkPWM Enable",
command=tkbtnPress, width=10)
tkBtn.grid(row=6, column=0, padx=10, pady=2)


tglBtn = Button(primaryFrame, text="Toggle tkrun",
command=tglbtnPress, width=10)
tglBtn.grid(row=7, column=0, padx=10, pady=2)


#Now start the GUI elements

tkpwm()                 #start the tk timer
root.mainloop()         #start window event loop
```

This block of code requires two buttons; otherwise, it affects the operation of others in the interface. The `tkbtnPress()` function changes the button text and sets a global variable to enable the functionality. The `tglbtnPress()` function toggles a global variable (`tkrun`) between `0` and `1` for on and off.

The `tkpwm()` function is called during the startup of the application and just before the `root.mainloop()` function. The timer calls itself by registering a `root.after()` timer and so runs continually in the background on a 50 ms timer. It looks at the `tkenable` and `tkrun` global variables to decide whether any `GPIO.output` calls are required. If `tkrun=1`, then the LED is on for 50 ms and off for 50 ms, giving a 10 Hz frequency and a 50 percent duty cycle.

# Block 7 – start the application

This code starts the TK timer loop and the main window message loop:

```
#Now start the GUI elements

tkpwm()                    #start the tk timer
root.mainloop()            #start window event loop
```

# TKinter switch demo

Since the action code for Python is so similar to that for TKinter, we will go directly to a TKinter interface for switch sensing. Since the plan is to eventually create push buttons for our Internet radio, let's show the breadboard schematic that we need to achieve this:

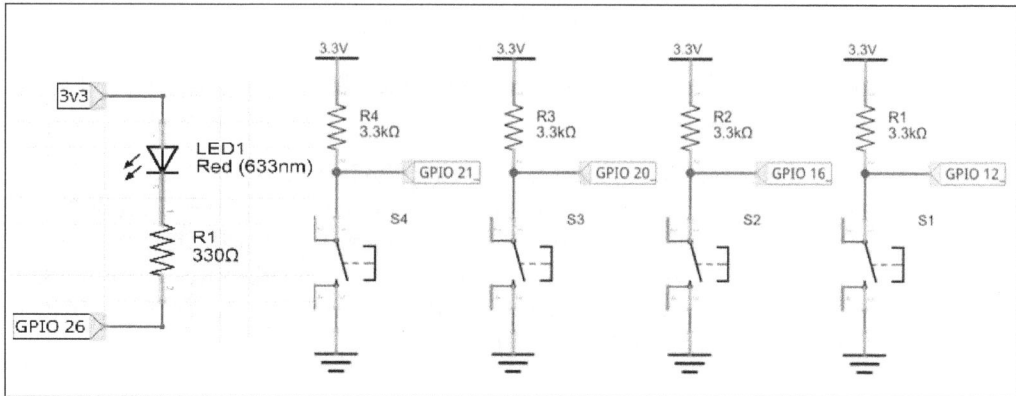

Warning: While the schematic shown is quite OK for breadboard use, it is not suitable where the wires to the switches are long (greater than a few inches). Notice that the GPIO pin would be exposed directly to any fault conditions. It is advisable to put at least a 1k Ohm series resistor to the GPIO pin. Never run the 5 Volt or 3.3 Volt supply through a long line to the switch (or LED location) as this directly exposes the supply to any potential wiring faults.

In preparation for the demo, complete the following:

1. Download the `tkswitch21.py` code from `http://1drv.ms/1ysAxkl`.

2. Store the `tkswitch21.py` file in `/home/pi/gpio`.

3. Run the code using IDLE3 by starting from a command line with `sudo idle3` (remember that we need superuser privileges to use `RPi.GPIO`).

The TKinter test GUI shows switch sensing using two different techniques, `GPIO.wait_for_edge(xx, ..)` and `GPIO.event_detected(xx)`, as shown in the following image:

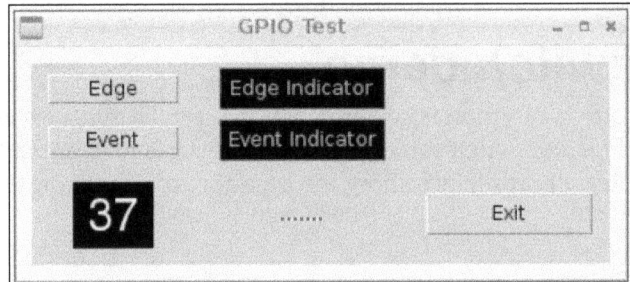

Once you have your switches set up and the code loaded into the development tool IDLE3, test the first switch:

- When you press the **Event** button, note that the button will stay depressed and you will see a message asking you to activate the switch (it's on BCM port 21). The seconds' timer is incrementing, showing that the interface is still responsive. When you then press the physical switch (S4 in the schematic), the LED and the Event indicator label will show the activity. Then the **Event** button will clear (back to the not-depressed state).

- When you now press the **Edge** button, the seconds timer stops, indicating that the interface has frozen. Press the physical switch (S4 in the schematic), and you will see the LED, label indicator, and message to press the button (really useful), and the seconds timer jumps to the current seconds count. This behavior is due to the fact that the code stops in the edge detection software.

The main action sections of the code are explained in the following section:

# Block 1 – the activity indicator

This code block implements a constant on-time (monostable) function for a single LED. You could use a similar implementation for many LEDs as the timers are maintained in a queue. The following is the code for the constant on-time function:

```
def monoLED(timer):
    if ( debug ): print("LED turned on")
    GPIO.output(26, 0)
    Rbvalue.set(0)
    root.after(timer, monotimeout)

def monotimeout():
    GPIO.output(26, 1)
    edgeidBtn.config(background="#000000")
    eventidBtn.config(background="#000000")
    Pvalue.set(value=".......")
```

This is a small pair of functions that shows the switch-pressing activity. The calling routines turn on the green background of the required **Edge/Event** indicator label, and call the monoLED(timevalue) function to turn on the LED and clear the label.

The monoLED(timevalue) function starts a root.after(mS) timer (in our case, it's 500 ms) that calls the monotimeout() function, which clears the LED and label indicators. This gives us a 500 ms monostable indicator when we press a switch.

# Block 2 – the Edge switch detector

This code is a great example of how not to implement switch sensing. To overcome the problem of the call blocking all other code execution in your application, you would have to implement multiple threads, which significantly increases the software complexity.

```
def edgebtnPress():
    if ( debug ): print ("Edge Button Pressed")
    Pvalue.set(value="Press the Button...")
    edgewait()

def edgewait():
    if ( debug ): print ("Edge wait start..")
    GPIO.setup(21, GPIO.IN, pull_up_down=GPIO.PUD_UP)
    GPIO.wait_for_edge(21, GPIO.FALLING, bouncetime=50)
    if ( debug ): print ("Edge detected..")
    GPIO.cleanup(21)
    edgeidBtn.config(background="#00FF00")
    monoLED(500)
```

The two functions in the preceding code handle the `wait_for_edge` method of switch sensing. The `edgebtnPress()` function is activated when you press the **Edge** button; it prints a couple of messages and calls the `edgewait()` function. The `edgewait()` function sets up the switch port pin as input and then stalls when the `GPIO.wait_for_edge()` call is executed. `RPi.GPIO` waits directly in its code and does not return until the call is fulfilled by an edge detect. This freezes the whole interface, whether it's Python or TKinter code, since it is running on the main thread of execution. Once the key sense occurs, the program continues. The TKinter GUI refreshes are slow enough for the **Press the Button..** label change not to have time to render before the thread is stalled. You will notice, however, that the console messages are shown.

> In this code, the `wait_for_edge` function has a bounce time of 50 ms specified. All mechanical switches have switch bounce, so you should always specify a suitable bounce time. Read up on switch bounce to understand how serious this problem can be; here is a good starting link:
>
> http://www.ganssle.com/debouncing.htm

Warning: We used an undocumented function in this code. The GPIO.cleanup() call is documented as resetting *ALL* the ports you have set up back to default state. However, this call will reset a specified port to default if used in this manner: GPIO.cleanup(21). Be aware that the behavior may change in future revisions. We tested this with version 0.5.11 of RPi.GPIO

# Block 3 – the Event switch detector

This code block shows a good way to implement switch sensing; using polling (as in this code) or using callbacks ensures a good user interface experience:

```
def eventbtnPress():
    if ( debug ): print ("Event Button Pressed")
    Pvalue.set(value="Press the Button...")
    GPIO.setup(21, GPIO.IN, pull_up_down=GPIO.PUD_UP)
    GPIO.add_event_detect(21, GPIO.FALLING, bouncetime=50)
    if ( debug ): print ("Waiting for event..")
    evwait()

def evwait():
    if GPIO.event_detected(21):
        if ( debug ): print ("Event detected...")
        GPIO.cleanup(21)
        eventidBtn.config(background="#00FF00")
        monoLED(500)
    else:
        root.after(20, evwait )
```

The two functions handle the event detector case. The eventbtnPress() function is called when you press the interface button. It programs the port for input and then calls the GPIO.add_event_detect() function to set up a non-blocking test of the switch (it does not stall the main thread and maintains the edge detection in its own code and threads). It then calls the evwait() function.

The evwait() function uses an if/else test to find out whether the switch has been activated. If it has been activated, it cleans the pin and shows the indicator. If the switch has not been activated yet, it sets up a root.after() timer of 20 ms to run the test again. It stays in this loop until the switch is activated but, since the timers are queued and maintained by TKinter, the interface is not blocked.

# Adding a physical switch interface to the Internet radio

Now that you have had the opportunity to experiment with sensing switches, we need to develop the code to add the external buttons to the Internet radio.

We will use four buttons, which are as follows:

- Two buttons for scrolling forward and backwards through the playlist using the Spinbox actions
- A button to select or start the playlist entry
- A button to stop the radio
- An LED to indicate each switch entry
- The mouse interface will still work

The code for adding a switch interface is encapsulated enough to provide a small demo of the buttons in action using IDLE3 before we combine the code.

The complete demo code is shown after the following paragraph. You have the option to type it in and then save it in a file you created, called /home/pi/gpio/ tkswitches.py. Or you can download the tkswitches.py code from http://1drv. ms/1ysAxkl.

The code opens an empty TKinter window when started and allows you to test all four buttons and the LED. The only console output is an LED turned on message when the LED flashes and the output identifying the BCM xx port when the switch action is on. The following is the complete demo code:

```
from tkinter import *
import RPi.GPIO as GPIO

indicator=False
debug=True

def setupswscan():
    GPIO.setmode(GPIO.BCM)
    GPIO.setup(26, GPIO.OUT, pull_up_down=GPIO.PUD_UP, initial=1)
    #LED, OFF
    for i in (21, 20, 16, 12):
        GPIO.setup(i, GPIO.IN, pull_up_down=GPIO.PUD_UP)
        #SW setup
```

```
            GPIO.add_event_detect(i, GPIO.FALLING, bouncetime=150)
        swscan()

def swscan():
    global indicator
    for i in (21, 20, 16, 12):
        #Test to see if there an event for each button
        if GPIO.event_detected(i):
            if i == 21:
                indicator=True
                if ( debug ): print("Detected BCM ", i)
                #playbtnPress()
            elif i == 20:
                indicator=True
                if ( debug ): print("Detected BCM ", i)
                #stopbtnPress()
            elif i == 16:
                indicator=True
                if ( debug ): print("Detected BCM ", i)
                #stationSpin.invoke("buttonup")
            elif i == 12:
                indicator=True
                if ( debug ): print("Detected BCM ", i)
                #stationSpin.invoke("buttondown")
            if indicator : monoLED(200)
    root.after(20, swscan )            #50Hz scan

def monoLED(timer):
    global indicator
    if ( debug ): print("LED turned on")
    if indicator and GPIO.input(26) :
        indicator=False
        GPIO.output(26, 0)
        root.after(timer, monotimeout)

def monotimeout():
    global indicator
    GPIO.output(26, 1)

root = Tk()                #Makes the root window

setupswscan()              #start scanning

root.mainloop()            #start window event loop
```

The code function operations are described in the following list:

- **Setupscan()**: This initializes the GPIO ports and adds event detection to each switch with a bounce time of 150 ms

- **Swscan()**: This tests each switch event maintained by `RPi.GPIO` to see whether an event has been detected. If there is an event from any port, then a flag call indicator is set. Notice here that the actual buttons that will be activated in the Internet radio UI are commented out here. At the end of event detection, if the indicator is `True`, then `monoLED(200)` is called to blink the LED for 200 ms. The call then registers a TK timer to call itself in 20 ms, so the switches are checked 50 times a second.

- **monoLED(timer)**: This turns the LED on if the indicator equals `True` and the LED port is high (LED off). Note here that, although GPIO 26 is configured as an output, you can still read the current logic level, which is very handy. If the LED GPIO 26 is low (on), then we don't try to blink it and simply exit leaving the indicator set so that 20 ms later, if the LED is then off, we will flash it again. This means that if you keep pressing buttons, the LED will flash continuously until you stop. When the LED is turned on, then the code also sets up the TK timer needed to turn the LED off in 200 ms.

- **monotimeout()**: This turns the LED off when the 200 ms TK timer ends.

- The last three immediate commands: create the TK window, start the switch scanning, and then start the window message loop.

The next step is to combine the switch-sensing code with the GUI code for the Internet radio; we'll use another, smaller test program to take this step:

- Download the `tkswtest.py` code from `http://1drv.ms/1ysAxkl`

- Store the files in `/home/pi/gpio`

- Run the file using IDLE3 by starting from a command line with `sudo idle3` (remember that we need superuser privileges to use `RPi.GPIO`)

The program `tkswtest.py` takes our integration one step further and replicates the complete Internet radio GUI with the switch detection added. The code does not yet have any of the functional radio logic in it, so it is simpler to read.

One change in the code is worth discussing. When initializing and building the GUI within the `buildwindow()` function, in the earlier implementation, we only needed to support mouse activation of the `stationSpin()` Spinbox control. Now, we need to allow switch activation to increment and decrement the Spinbox focus.

We enable this by declaring `stationSpin` to be global, as shown in the following snippet:

```
global stationSpin
stationSpin=Spinbox(subFrame, width=25,…
stationSpin.config( font=("Helvetica", 22),…
stationSpin.grid()
```

The `stationSpin` reference acts very much like a variable, although in this case it's actually a class reference. Since all the class references inside the `buildwindow()` definition are local, we cannot access them unless we make this global declaration.

Now, within the `swscan()` definition, we can access the `stationSpin` control using `stationSpin.invoke` to trigger `buttonup` and `buttondown` actions, as shown in the following code:

```
def swscan():
    global indicator
    for i in (21, 20, 16, 12):
        #Test to see if there an event for each button
        if GPIO.event_detected(i):
            if i == 21:
                indicator=True
                playbtnPress()
            elif i == 20:
                indicator=True
                stopbtnPress()
            elif i == 16:
                indicator=True
                stationSpin.invoke("buttonup")
            elif i == 12:
                indicator=True
                stationSpin.invoke("buttondown")
            if indicator : monoLED(200)
    root.after(20, swscan )
```

# Project 1 – Add a switch interface to the Internet radio

Now that we have seen the code to implement the external switch/LED actions and integrated that with a basic TKinter GUI, we can show the final result. The program is close to 300 lines long, but we hope that having incrementally added functionality, you can read through it with relative ease.

To start this project:

- Download the `swradio.py` code file from `http://1drv.ms/1ysAxk1`.
- Save the file in `/home/pi/radio/bin`.
- You can run the program `swradio.py` in IDLE3 to see the console output, but remember to use a command prompt to start IDLE3 as the root (`sudo idle3`). The window interface still works but, in addition, you can now use the buttons to navigate, start, and stop the stations.

There are many workarounds for setting permissions and groups to give root access required for the `RPi.GPIO`; however, the following set of instructions simply start the application (`swradio.py`) using a root instance of Python 3 when the desktop starts.

To set up the `swradio.py` file to start when the desktop starts, perform the following steps:

1. Using File Manager, open the `/home/pi/.config` folder (you can use *Ctrl + H* to show hidden files and folders).
2. Create a new folder called `lxsession`.
3. In the `lxsession` folder, create a folder called `LXDE-pi`.
4. In the `LXDE-pi` folder, create a blank file called `autostart`.
5. Edit `/home/pi/.config/lxsession/LXDE-pi/autostart` in Leafpad.
6. Enter the following lines of text:
   ```
   @sudo /usr/bin/python3
   /home/pi/radio/bin/swradio.py
   ```
7. Save the file.
8. Log out and then log in as user `pi`

The Internet radio should load automatically after the desktop is started. This `autostart` file is only for the user `pi`. There is a non user-specific file that applies to all users at `/etc/xdg/lxsession/LXDE-pi/autostart`. Any changes you add to this file apply to any users who logon to the Pi.

 You can turn off the window title bar by right-clicking on the title bar and selecting **Un/Decorate**. To re-enable the title bar, hover the mouse pointer over the top or bottom edge of the window, right-click, and select **Un/Decorate** again.

If you examine the listing for `swradio.py`, you will see that the additional code is identical to that just used in `switches.py`. The listing is now about as long as you would want to have as a monolithic application (about 300 lines of code).

We now have three functional versions of the Internet radio:

- `swradio.py`: This file is specifically a Pi implementation since it now includes RPi.GPIO. This application can, however, talk to a remote instance of VLC, and that instance could be running on a Raspberry Pi, PC or Mac (it uses Telnet to talk to VLC).

- `tkradio.py`: This file is generic enough to be run using Python 3 on a Raspberry Pi, a PC running Windows, or a Mac .

- `radio.py`: This file is a simple Python text mode interface that should be easy to implement cross-platform.

In addition, the instructions you have for configuring VLC should be generic enough that it could be fully implemented on any platform with just the remote user interface on the Raspberry Pi.

# Summary

Now that we've completed the fifth chapter, let's review some of the main tasks you learned how to do:

- Driving LEDs and sensing switches using digital I/O ports and unearthing the potential problems and restrictions that apply to their use

- Adding a switch interface with an activity indicator LED to the Internet radio project from *Chapter 4, Raspberry Pi Audio Input and Output*

In the next chapter, you will start to exercise some of the Raspberry Pi input and output ports to drive RC-servos over the I2C (SMBUS) interface.

# 6
# Driving I2C Peripherals on the Raspberry Pi

In the previous chapter, we tested the single-bit digital I/O ports built into the Raspberry Pi SOC. Now it's time to shift gears to another built-in interface for hardware interfaces.

In this chapter, we will talk about an interface bus that uses a simple message communication protocol that communicates from a master device to a slave device. You will see this referred to as I2C (pronounced I-squared-C) and sometimes as **(System Management Bus) SMBus** in most Pi technical documentation. Each has different capabilities, but they are essentially identical in protocol. For our needs, we will treat the names as interchangeable, but to be more accurate—we will use I2C.

After completing this chapter, you will be able to:

- Understand the characteristics of the I2C protocol and its peripheral addressing scheme
- Read and write to interfaces on the I2C bus
- Create a program to control a multichannel PWM controller

## Getting started with I2C

The specifications for both I2C and SMBus are quite complex. For more in-depth documentation on the differences between I2C and SMBus, refer to the following resources:

- http://smbus.org/specs/index.html
- http://www.nxp.com/documents/user_manual/UM10204.pdf

The I2C bus is a shared-media multi-drop architecture with only two lines: (1) serial data (SDA) and (2) serial clock (SCL) – not including the ground. The bus is in a quiescent state when no transactions are being sent or received and both the SDA and SCL lines are pulled high by resistors to 3.3V in the Pi (or 5V in other implementations). The master and slave devices only ever pull the data line low, which is described as a wired OR connection. The following diagram shows the general I2C architecture and its location on the Pi I/O connector. Pins 3 and 5 can also be used as GPIO ports but not while you have I2C enabled, so you lose two GPIO ports.

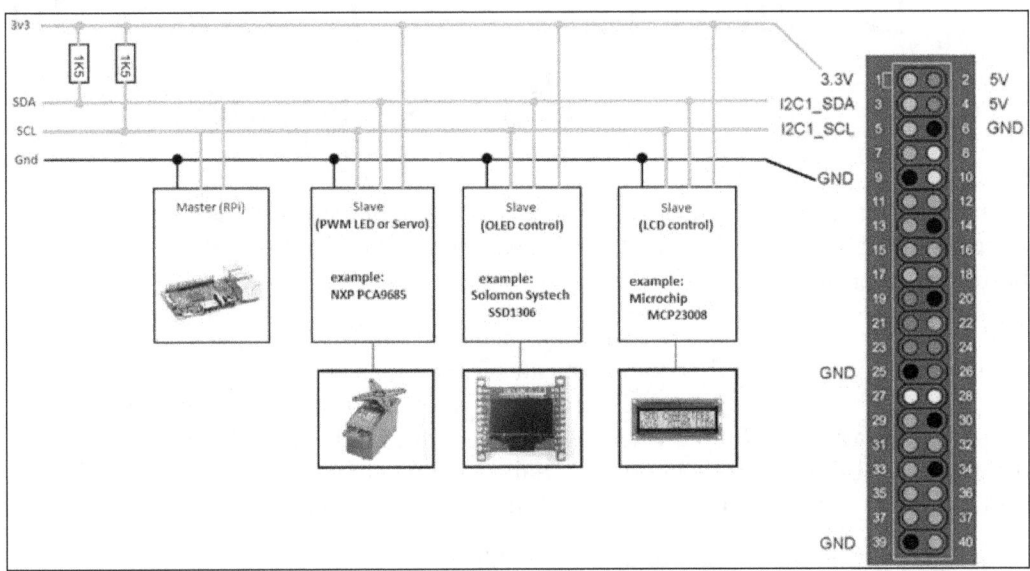

At the protocol level, I2C is similar in concept to the RS232 serial; there is a start condition and a stop condition specified, and the start condition synchronizes the receiver with the sender. In the case of I2C, there is always a multi-byte transaction to send or receive data, and the master is always in charge. The slaves never initiate transactions; they only respond to requests from the master.

When the master initiates a transaction and data transfer to or from a slave, it is a multi- byte, byte-by-byte transfer that, in most simple cases, consists of:

- A start indicator
- An address field that allows a single slave to respond
- An ACK (acknowledge) from the addressed slave for its address

- A register address (or word address) for a particular storage location in the slave

- At least one byte of data for the addressed location

- An ACK from the master or slave, depending on whether it's a read or write

- A stop indicator

One very simple I2C device that is very commonly used on the Pi is the **Maxim DS1307 Real Time Clock (RTC)**. This is an eight-pin IC with a fixed slave address (so you can only have one on your I2C bus) and an array of 64 read/write registers. Registers 0x0–0x7 are the RTC functions and 0x8–0x3F are spare RAM. The device provides a battery-backed RTC function, so you don't need to go to the Internet to find out the time. You can search for the datasheet for this device online or download it from `http://1drv.ms/1ysAxkl`.

Please note that numbers specified as 0x??, such as 0xFF are hex numbers. Each digit represents 4 bits. So, two hex digits represent 8 bits, and so on. Each hex value can be 0, 1, 2, 3, 4, 5, 6, 7, 8, 9, A, B, C, D, E or F representing the 4-bit field. The following image shows a write transaction for the DS1307:

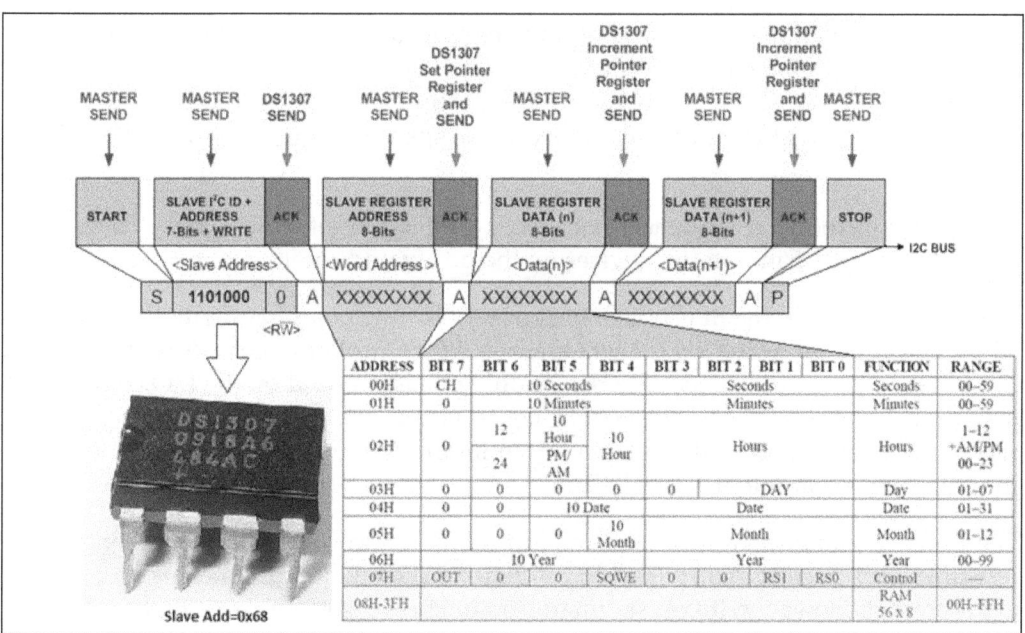

| ADDRESS | BIT 7 | BIT 6 | BIT 5 | BIT 4 | BIT 3 | BIT 2 | BIT 1 | BIT 0 | FUNCTION | RANGE |
|---|---|---|---|---|---|---|---|---|---|---|
| 00H | CH | 10 Seconds | | | Seconds | | | | Seconds | 00–59 |
| 01H | 0 | 10 Minutes | | | Minutes | | | | Minutes | 00–59 |
| 02H | 0 | 12 | 10 Hour | 10 Hour | Hours | | | | Hours | 1–12 +AM/PM |
| | | 24 | PM/ AM | | | | | | | 00–23 |
| 03H | 0 | 0 | 0 | 0 | 0 | DAY | | | Day | 01–07 |
| 04H | 0 | 0 | 10 Date | | Date | | | | Date | 01–31 |
| 05H | 0 | 0 | 0 | 10 Month | Month | | | | Month | 01–12 |
| 06H | 10 Year | | | | Year | | | | Year | 00–99 |
| 07H | OUT | 0 | 0 | SQWE | 0 | 0 | RS1 | RS0 | Control | — |
| 08H-3FH | | | | | | | | | RAM 56 x 8 | 00H–FFH |

Proceeding from left to right, the following are the steps involved in the transaction shown in the preceding image

1. The master sends a start signal.

2. The master sends the slave the I2C bus address and the R/W bit (0=write).

3. The slave, if present, sends an ACK back to the master so that the master knows it is there.

4. The master sends the register address (often described as the word address).

5. The slave sends an ACK message for each byte written and internally auto-increments its register pointer to the next register in its set.

6. The master sends a stop signal to end the transaction.

A read transaction is very similar except that the master generates the ACK for each data byte it receives from the slave.

You might be puzzled by this as there is nothing in the transaction that indicates how many bytes are being sent. The master simply keeps sending clocks to request or transfer more data.

The last thing to know is the speed of transfer (the clock frequency) for a transaction. I2C originally specified a maximum rate of 100 kHz; this was later raised to 400 kHz, and again to 1.7 Mhz and 3.4 Mhz. The SMBus specifies operation from a much lower 10 kHz to 100 kHz. In the Pi the I2C clock speed is set to a nominal 100 kHz by default.

SMBus also introduced the concept of a clock-initiated reset, where, if the clock line was held low for 35 ms, all the devices on the bus would reset.

The I2C controller in the Pi is not an SMBus and is fully compliant with the NXP I2C 2.1 specification up to 400 kHz. There are two I2C controllers called Broadcom Serial Control (BSC 0, 1) implemented in the Pi; only one is exposed on the I/O connector (I2C-1 on the later Pi's). A second controller is used for the HDMI connection and allows the transfer and control of display configuration information (I2C-0). You should never attempt to use this I2C port.

The Raspberry Pi does not include a real-time clock, and we are not developing a real-time clock project in our *Raspberry Pi Essentials* book because there is little need to program it. However, if you are interested in knowing more about real-time clocks (RTC), a simple Internet search will provide you with heaps of information on installing an I2C-RTC solution. If you are permanently connected to the Internet, you don't need an RTC as you can get the time from a time server (NNTP).

# Understanding address fields

While the standards for I2C 7-bit addressing are clear, it can be challenging at times to understand addressing as implemented within software libraries.

You should always think of I2C's 7-bit address in this way:

The address and the R/W signal make up an 8-bit field. However, some vendors and software developers incorrectly specify the address as 8 bits, using the R/W signal as part of the address. When described in this manner, they typically use the two hex digits as the address and consider even addresses as writes and odd addresses as reads. In the following example, the correct I2C peripheral address is 0x68 (the RTC chip address), but you might see it shown as writes to 0xD2 or reads from 0xD3:

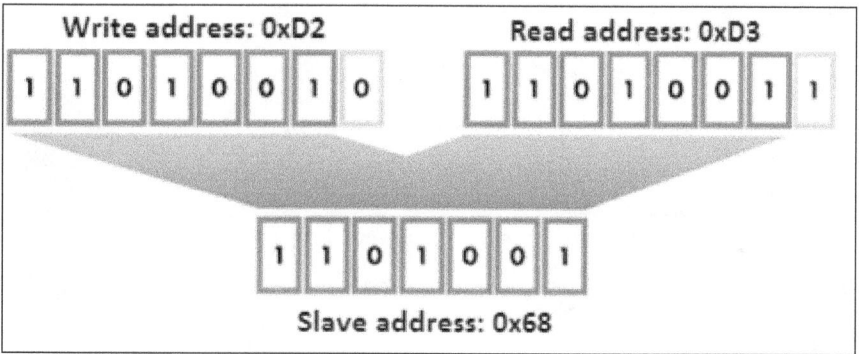

# Driving RC servos

To prepare for our robot project in *Chapter 8, Creating a Raspberry Pi Lane Following Robot*, we need to take a small diversion into motor control and RC servos. Robotic projects tend to use DC motors with a feedback sensor as the main drive mechanism. In our case, the robot's power and speed requirements are less demanding. Two modified analog RC servos with an encapsulated motor, gearbox, and control system are well within our requirements.

Most RC servos are designed to rotate the output shaft only about 180 degrees. They are driven by a pulse width modulated signal that controls the angular position of the servo. Servos modified for continuous rotation set their clockwise or counterclockwise speed based on the same pulse width modulated signals.

If you'd like to compare a DC motor/sensor with a continuous rotation servo, refer to the following resources:

- Parallax (`http://www.parallax.com/sites/default/files/downloads/900-00008-Continuous-Rotation-Servo-Documentation-v2.2.pdf`): This servo works from 4–6 VDC and produces about 38 oz-inch of torque. It draws under 200 mA at maximum torque, but this increases to about 500 mA or more if stalled. This is the servo we will use in the robot project.

- Servo City (`https://www.servocity.com/html/52_rpm_planetary_gearmotor_w__.html`): This DC servo works from 3–12 VDC and produces about 290 oz-inch of torque. The stall current is almost 5 A.

The following image shows the operational voltage range and the direction of the spindle caused by the pulse width (time period) of the drive signal in a servo motor:

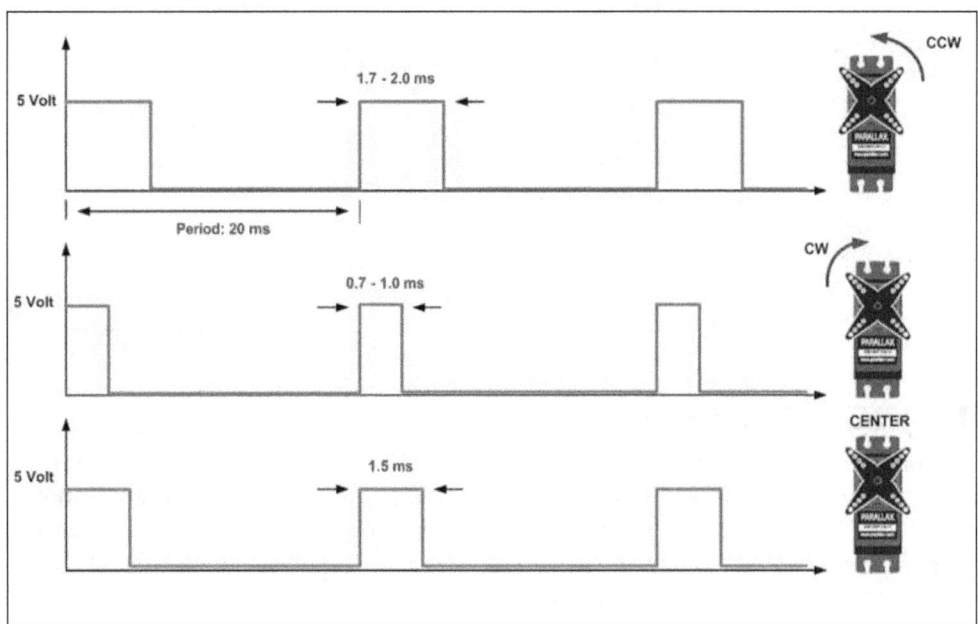

In the preceding image, a 1.5 ms pulse width signal repeated at least every 20 ms is called the neutral or center position. For a continuous rotation servo, neutral is stopped. As the pulse width increases, the servo turns counterclockwise; as it decreases, the servo moves clockwise (looking at the front of the servo). As these servos use analog circuitry, this means that very small changes in the pulse width don't necessarily move the servo. This is described as a deadband and might vary from just a few microseconds to more than 20 μs depending on the servo and load torque required. This deadband limits the maximum resolution you can get from a servo. For example, if you had a 180-degree servo with a 1 ms (1.0–2.0 ms) PWM range, then you would need a definite response to a 5.5 μs change in pulse width to achieve a 1 degree resolution. A 20 μs deadband might limit small-step response to about 4 degrees. To compare digital and analog deadband, refer to the `http://www.futaba-rc.com/servos/digitalservos.pdf` Futaba paper.

The 20 ms (50 Hz) repeat rate of the control pulse is called the frame rate; if this falls much below 50 Hz, the servo stops driving. This is called *freewheeling*, and in this state, no power is applied to the internal motor. So, in summary, to keep our servo working, we must meet the following three PWM input signal requirements:

1. A pulse width signal between 0.5 ms and 2.5 ms (this is more than that shown in the previous image, but many servos work out to this range) to exercise the full range of position/speed available.
2. A 1.5 ms signal for a neutral position or zero speed.
3. A fixed frame rate for the signal, that is, => 50 Hz. Most servos work well in the 50–70 Hz range.

One last issue to discuss about servos; those that we have previously shown are analog servos and are the lowest cost versions. There are digital-controlled servos that contain a small computer controller, and they can cost considerably more. These respond to the same 0.5 ms to 2.5 ms pulse width but use a frame rate of about 300 Hz which, allied with the digital control, provide a much higher performance.

# Raspberry Pi software requirements for SMBus

Now, back to I2C, we need to configure our Pi to enable I2C operation and get the basic software to drive the bus.

To enable I2C operation, perform the following steps:

1.  Perform an `apt-get update/upgrade/autoremove` cycle to make sure you have not missed any important updates to your system before you install any new software.

2.  Use File Manager in root mode (open a new window with root privileges), find the file `/etc/modprobe.d/raspi-blacklist.conf`, right-click on it, and open it in Leafpad.

3.  Add a comment (#) in front of the following line:

    `i2c-bcm2708 becomes #i2c-bcm2708`

4.  This can also be done using the `raspi-config` command to enable I2C, so the line may already be commented out as we enabled I2C during our install in *Chapter 1*, *Getting Started with Raspberry Pi*.

5.  Use File Manager in root mode (open a new window with root privileges), find the file `/etc/modules`, right-click on it, and open it in Leafpad.

6.  Add the following two entry lines to the `/etc/modules` file:

    ◦  `i2c-bcm2708`

    ◦  `i2c-dev`

7.  Close the file after saving the changes.

8.  From a command line, type `sudo apt-get install -y python-smbus`.

9.  From a command line, type `sudo apt-get install -y i2c-tools`.

10. From a command line, type `sudo adduser pi i2c`.

    This gives the owner permissions to `/dev/i2c-1`

11. Reboot your Raspberry Pi.

We now have all the software required to talk to devices on the I2C bus. On the hardware side, we will use an Adafruit I2C 16-Channel PWM board that uses an **NXP PCA9685** I2C chip. I'll use this to drive two Parallax continuous rotation servos.

Both items are available from the Adafruit website; see the following links:

- `http://www.adafruit.com/product/154`
- `http://www.adafruit.com/product/815`

The following image shows the Adafruit board before installing the I/O connectors:

The features of the board are as follows:

- 6 bits of address selection allowing up to 62 boards to be connected
- Programmable to drive analog (50–70 Hz) and digital (300 Hz+) servos
- 220 Ohm series resistors in PWM lines provide output current limiting and so can be used to drive indicator LEDs without the need for external current limiting resistors.
- Reverse voltage protection on the V+ line

> The PCA9685 is powered directly from the VCC line, which will be the Raspberry Pi's 3.3 V supply. Do not connect VCC to the Pi's 5V supply. The V+ supply is used only for the servos and can be 5–6 V. Do not connect servos to the Pi's 5V supply; a stalled servo can draw excessive current, so always power servos separately. Great caution must be taken to avoid shorting points on the board and wiring. For example, shorting V+ to VCC or the data/clock line could blow up your Raspberry Pi and unfortunately VCC and V+ are on adjacent pins.

Here's what your breadboard build might look like with the servo V+ supplied by an external battery pack:

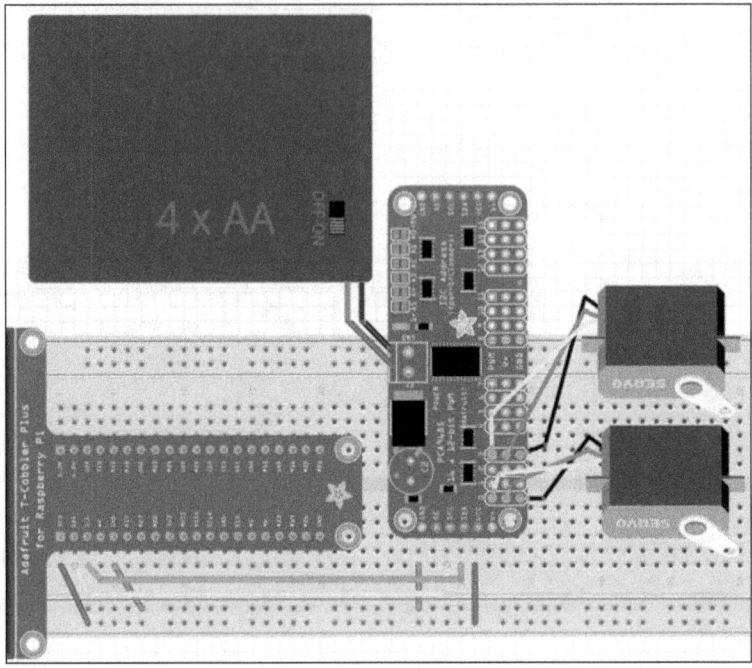

If you have the 16-Channel PWM board hooked up to the Raspberry Pi, we can at last test it to see whether the board responds. The I2C tools utility called **i2cdetect** will catalogue all devices on the I2C bus by sending address and data bytes and seeing whether there is an ACK response from a device.

From an LXterminal command prompt, type the following:

1.  `sudo i2cdetect -l`: This is used to display the active I2C buses on the computer. This may show `i2c-0` and `i2c-1` on the early Raspberry Pis.

2.  `sudo i2cdetect -y 1`: This is used to probe slave addresses to test whether a slave interface exists. You may have to use bus 0 on early Raspberry Pis.

3.  `sudo i2cdetect -F 1`: This is used to probe the capabilities of the driver/master for the bus.

The following is the output image of the command `sudo i2cdetect -l` for our system:

```
                              pi@raspberrypi: ~                          _ □ ×
 File  Edit  Tabs  Help
 pi@raspberrypi ~ $ sudo i2cdetect -l
 i2c-1    i2c                 bcm2708_i2c.1                    I2C adapter
 pi@raspberrypi ~ $ sudo i2cdetect 1
 WARNING! This program can confuse your I2C bus, cause data loss and worse!
 I will probe file /dev/i2c-1.
 I will probe address range 0x03-0x77.
 Continue? [Y/n] y
       0  1  2  3  4  5  6  7  8  9  a  b  c  d  e  f
 00:           -- -- -- -- -- -- -- -- -- -- -- -- --
 10: -- -- -- -- -- -- -- -- -- -- -- -- -- -- -- --
 20: -- -- -- -- -- -- -- -- -- -- -- -- -- -- -- --
 30: -- -- -- -- -- -- -- -- -- -- -- -- 3c -- -- --
 40: 40 -- -- -- -- -- -- -- -- -- -- -- -- -- -- --
 50: -- -- -- -- -- -- -- -- -- -- -- -- -- -- -- --
 60: -- -- -- -- -- -- -- -- -- -- -- -- -- -- -- --
 70: 70 -- -- -- -- -- --
 pi@raspberrypi ~ $ sudo i2cdetect -F 1
 Functionalities implemented by /dev/i2c-1:
 I2C                              yes
 SMBus Quick Command              yes
 SMBus Send Byte                  yes
 SMBus Receive Byte               yes
 SMBus Write Byte                 yes
 SMBus Read Byte                  yes
 SMBus Write Word                 yes
 SMBus Read Word                  yes
 SMBus Process Call               yes
 SMBus Block Write                yes
 SMBus Block Read                 no
 SMBus Block Process Call         no
 SMBus PEC                        yes
 I2C Block Write                  yes
 I2C Block Read                   yes
 pi@raspberrypi ~ $ █
```

In the preceding image, you can see that we have only a single I2C bus (i2c-1) exposed. Multiple devices show on the slave map (0x3c, 0x40 and 0x70) as well as a list of the commands supported by the driver/master for bus 1. The PWM board actually responds to two I2C addresses—0x40 and 0x70.

> There are multiple reserved addresses in the lower I2C address range. The listing shows that the addresses 0, 1, and 2 are not specifically probed. However, you should not see any devices below 0x20.

# Programming the PCA 9685 to drive a servo

The datasheet for the PCA9685 can be sourced from the Internet or downloaded from our `Chapter 6` folder at `http://1drv.ms/1ysAxkl`

Don't be put off by the size of the datasheet (51 pages); we only need to understand the basic functionality of the chip and a subset of the registers used to program it. We'll refer to section numbers and table figure references in the version we provided to help you.

The first point to be made is that the chip was not designed to specifically drive servos; it was produced for the control of the LCD backlight LEDs in laptops. However, the brightness control in this application is a PWM function, so it can be useful anywhere an accurate PWM is needed.

The major PCA 9685 programmable features of interest to the servo application are:

- The frame rate for the PWM is adjustable from 40–1000 Hz with the internal clock. This is well within our requirements to drive both analog and digital servos.

  We will set this to 60 Hz for our analog servo. The formula for the pre-scale divider count is given in Datasheet (7.3.5) and for 60 Hz, it is 101 (0x65)

- The PWM on and off times are adjustable over 4,096 steps and programmed for each channel, as given in Datasheet (7.3.3). This range covers the whole frame time of 16.6 ms, so the discrete step size for the pulse is approximately 4 µs. In our application, our pulse width might vary from a minimum of 0.5 ms through to 2.5 ms maximum. This will represent pulse width counts of approximately 123 to 616, with our neutral point at a count of 370, as shown in the following diagram:

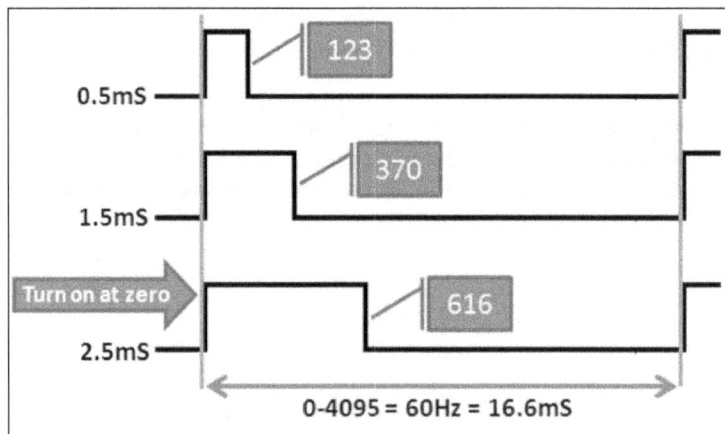

# PCA 9685 addressing and registers

The PCA 9685 powers on with a prescribed set of defaults. The device can also be sent a software reset (SWRST) that sets it to the same power-on conditions.

By default, the PWM board is addressed as 0x40 on the I2C bus. To move to a different address, you have to solder contacts on the board.

The device has a large number of registers, but we are only interested in the following:

- **MODE1** (Datasheet Table 3 and 7.3.1): This provides all the control functions needed to configure I2C and control the frame rate, auto increment, power state, and so on.

- **LEDxx** (Datasheet Table 3): There are 16 (one for each channel) sets of 4 (6–69) registers that provide the low and high byte pairs for each of the 12-bit on and off count settings for the output pulse. By default, the chip activates new pulse width settings on detecting a stop signal after a write. If you write to these registers with individual transactions, the pulse width will update after each write. This could result in spurious pulse widths as you update each member of the value pair. To get around this, we will write all four registers in a single transaction. This ensures that all four registers are written before the pulse width is updated.

- **ALL_LED** (Datasheet Table 3): The four registers at location 250–253 are special on and off count registers that program all the channels simultaneously. These will be used to initialize the channels and set them all to neutral (1.5ms) with a single write transaction.

- **PRE_SCALE** (Datasheet Table 3): This is a single register that holds the divider value for the frame frequency. This can only be set while the chip is in sleep mode (bit 4 in the MODE1 register is set).

# Project 1 – Python control of a PWM board driving RC servo motors

You should now have a reasonable understanding of what is required to program an I2C PWM board, so let's look at some Python code to drive the Adafruit 16 channel PWM board.

 The python-smbus library is compatible only with Python 2 at the time of writing. To run PCA9685, you have to use IDLE and not IDLE3. To run from the command line, use Python and not Python 3. As with the `RPi-GPIO` library, the SMBus library needs to have root privileges.

First, create a new /home/pi/servo project directory for the files and download pca9685.py from the Chapter 6 folder at http://1drv.ms/1ysAxkl into the directory.

Then, open the pca9685.py file in the idle development environment, remembering to use the sudo idle command to start it.

## Code block 1 – imports, constants, and variables

In this code block, we import the minimum amount for our functionality. Note here that the bus number i2c-1 or i2c-0 may vary depending on the Raspberry Pi version you have. Check the output of the i2cdetect -l command to discover which one to use. Here's code block 1:

```python
#!/usr/bin/python

from time import sleep
from random import randrange
from smbus import SMBus

# ============================================================
# With help from Adafruit PCA9685 16-Channel PWM Servo Driver
# ============================================================

# RPi - PCA9685 Constants
__i2cbus            = 0x01      #older Pi may use bus 0 = 0x00
__Gencall           = 0x00
```

```
__PCA9685add        = 0x40
__PCA9685rst        = 0x06      #GenCall(0x06) resets all PCA9685
__MODE1             = 0x00
__PRESCALE          = 0xFE
__LED0_ON_L         = 0x06      #first register in quad
__Neutral           = [ 0x00, 0x00, 0x72, 0x01 ]   #1.5mS=370=0x172
__Quadlen           = 0x04

#create i2c SMBus object reference
i2c = SMBus(__i2cbus)
```

# Code block 2 – I2C access functions

This code block defines the functions that call the I2C library. Each call uses a `try:`/`except:` block to ensure we catch any errors that might occur. This code is generic but incudes only the library functions we need for this application:

```
def busWritebyte( address, reg):
    #Adresses a single special register
    try:
        return i2c.write_byte(address, reg)
    except IOError, err:
        if debug : print "Error on byte write ",
address, reg, err
        return True


def busReadbytedata (address, reg ):
    #Reads a single bye from a register
    try:
        return i2c.read_byte_data(address, reg)
    except IOError, err :
        if debug : print "IO Error busreadbytedata ",
address, reg, err
        return True


def busWritebytedata (address, reg, data):
    #Writes a single byte to a register
    try:
        i2c.write_byte_data(address, reg, data)
        return False
```

```
        except IOError, err :
            if debug : print "IO Error buswritebyte ",
    address, reg, data, err
            return True


    def busWritelist(address, reg, alist):
        #Writes an array of bytes in a list (needs AI)
        try:
            i2c.write_i2c_block_data(address, reg, alist)
            return False
        except IOError, err :
            if debug : print "IO Error buswritelist ",
    address, reg, alist, err
            return True


    def busReadlist(address, reg, listlen):
        #Read multiple bytes into an array (needs AI)
        try:
            return i2c.read_i2c_block_data(address, reg, listlen)
        except IOError, err :
            if debug : print "IO Error buswritelist ",
    address, reg, listlen, err
            return True
```

These definitions perform the I2C reads and writes:

- `busWritebyte( address, reg)`: This is used to talk to special function registers, such as `GenCall(0x06)`, that can be used to reset all the PCA9685 chips at once

- `busReadbytedata(address, reg )` and `busWritebytedata (address, reg, data)`: These are used to read/write a single byte to a defined register

- `busReadlist(address, reg, listlen)` and `busWritelist(address, reg, alist)`: These functions read or write `python list[]` in a single transaction, and the interface supports a maximum of 32 bytes per transaction

The documentation for the Python-SMBus module is sparse, but refer to `http://wiki.erazor-zone.de/wiki:linux:python:smbus:doc` for an overview.

# Code block 3 – the PCA9685 specific code

This code block contains all the specific logic required to drive this particular I2C chip. For the PCA9685, since the AI functionality is required, here is where we verify that the chip is correctly configured. If you were designing a method to drive a unique interface, this is where you would create your own particular software embodiment. Here's code block 3:

```
def PCA9685_reset():
    try:
        busWritebyte(__Gencall, __PCA9685rst)
        return False
    except:
        print "Exception error"
        return True


def setPWMFreq(freq):
    # Sets the PWM frequency for this board
    prescale = 25000000.0       #25MHz rc osc
    prescale /= 4096.0          #12-bit resolution
    prescale /= float(freq)
    prescale -= 1.0
    prescale = int(prescale + 0.5)
    # the PCA9685 must be asleep to set the prescale divider count
    try:
        mode1data = busReadbytedata(__PCA9685add, __MODE1)
    #read current MODE1 reg
        if not (mode1data & 0x10) :
            mode1data = mode1data | 0x10
    # sleep bit not set
            busWritebytedata(__PCA9685add, __MODE1, mode1data)
    #MODE1 write sleep
        busWritebytedata(__PCA9685add, __PRESCALE, prescale)
    #write prescale count
        mode1data=mode1data & 0xEF | 0x20
    #MODE1 set AI, clear SLEEP
        busWritebytedata(__PCA9685add, __MODE1, mode1data)
    #MODE1 write
```

```
        sleep(0.001)      #wait time for osc
        return False
    except:
        print "Exception error"
        return True


def setPWMquad(address, channel, alist):
    # Sets a single PWM channel, count can be 0-4095
    # Channels are 0-15 for individual settings and 61
    # for ALL_LED_ON_L
    # Quad register List is [ON_lsb, ON_msb, OFF_lsb, OFF_msb]
    try:
        busWritelist(address, __LED0_ON_L + 4 * channel, alist )
        return False
    except:
        print "Exception error"
        return True


def getPWMquad(address, channel, length):
    # Gets a single PWM channel values
    # Channels are 0-15 for individual settings and 61
    # returns [0,0,0,0]
    # Quad register List is [ON_lsb, ON_msb, OFF_lsb, OFF_msb]
    try:
        return busReadlist(address, __LED0_ON_L + 4 * channel,
            length )
    except:
        print "Exception error"
        return True
```

These functions are the PCA9685-specific code that provides the following:

- PCA9685_reset (): This uses the GenCall special function register to do a software reset

- setPWMFreq (freq): This calculates the pre-scale divider for the required frequency, puts the chip to sleep, and updates and enables the frame clock. Note that the code sets the AI bit, and this is specific to this chip.

- setPWMquad(address, channel, alist): This writes a list[] of values to a register set (4 registers) defining the on and off values for the pulse width on a given channel. We don't check AI here since we have to perform setPWMfreq(xx) to have a valid frame rate.

- getPWMquad(address, channel, length): This is not actually used in our code but included for completeness. This function reads a register set of four values defining the pulse width for a given channel. We don't check AI here since we have to perform setPWMfreq(xx) to have a valid frame rate.

# Code block 4: the test code

This code block is a simple test of the PWM. All the complexity of the interface is hidden in the previously defined blocks, leaving only simple errors to be caught in this block Here's the test code block:

```
def main():
    print "Starting Test on channels 0-7"

    PCA9685_reset()

    setPWMFreq(60)

    #Set neutral on all channels using register 61, (0xFA)
    setPWMquad(__PCA9685add, 61, __Neutral)
    while True:
        try:
            sleep (0.100)
            newquad= [0,0, randrange(250, 500, 4),randrange(0, 3,
1)]

            newchan= randrange(0, 8, 1)
            setPWMquad(__PCA9685add, newchan, newquad)
        except KeyboardInterrupt:
            print "Keyboard Interrupt"
            setPWMquad(__PCA9685add, 61, __Neutral)
            break

main()
```

This code does a software reset, initializes the clock, and sets all the channels to neutral. Note here that the code writes to register 61 (0xFA), which is the special register quad that writes to all channel quads simultaneously. The small main() endless loop writes random values (updates at about a 10 Hz rate) in the 1–2 ms range on channels 0–7 while 8–15 are at neutral. You can exit the program using *Ctrl + C*.

The longest I2C transaction (quad register read/write) in the code takes less than 60 µs to perform. With this throughput, it should be possible to update many hundreds of servos at a high rate without problems. The only peripherals likely to be a challenge at the default 100 kHz bus clock speed may be high-density OLED and LCD screens.

 On a cautionary note, if you are experimenting with this code using normal (non-continuous rotation) servos, make sure to understand the maximum/minimum pulse width your servos can accept. Driving conventional servos into their mechanical end stops can result in excess current being drawn or even damage to the servo.

## Other demo code

We have deliberately kept our project code simple and easy to read. In your search to learn more about these types of projects with your Pi, you will find lots of code and hardware available with greater functionality and abstraction using class-based software design.

Consider exploring some of the I2C peripherals and code available from http://adafruit.com (also available from http://thepihut.com/); they are easy to work through. Take for example the 8x8 and 24 LED Bargraph I2C displays shown in the following image:

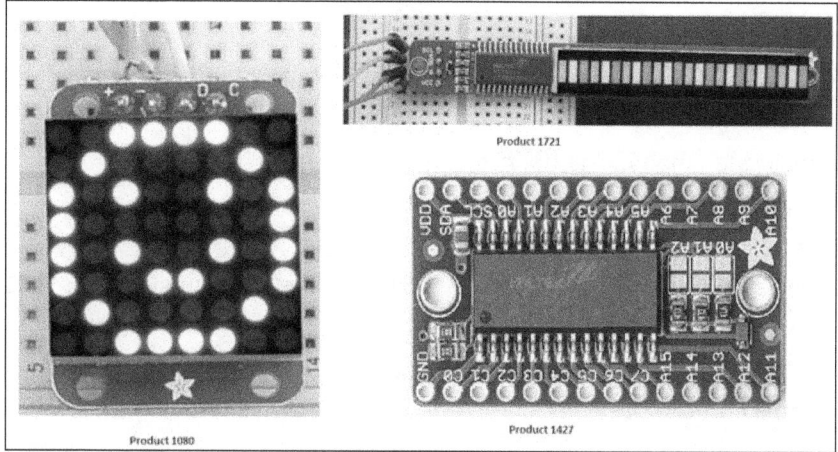

Product 1721

Product 1080

Product 1427

Adafruit, like many other suppliers, provides learning resources, drivers, and example code that can help you understand the topic further. For the displays shown in the preceding image, visit `https://learn.adafruit.com/matrix-7-segment-led-backpack-with-the-raspberry-pi/configuring-your-pi-for-i2c` for a discussion on hardware and software installation for these displays.

The Holtek HT 16K33 used in these displays is another great example of an I2C peripheral, which, like the PCA9685, makes use of register auto-increment to simplify data transfer. The class libraries provided by Adafruit are good examples of what can be achieved. One thing to note is that the code provided is liberally sprinkled with console print statements and you can speed update considerably by removing these.

Now that you've completed this chapter, you have a better understanding of I2C hardware and software, along with a deep dive into device datasheets and RC servos. This model will enable you to:

- Design software solutions that use I2C as implemented in the Pi to interface with external functions. This type of connection interface is useful for a range of device functions, such as the RTC, PWM, extended digital I/O, accelerometer, compass, and GPS module.

- Inspect datasheets for I2C interface chips and derive a method of controlling the chip functions from your applications.

- Choose and apply RC servos for a project.

# Summary

Now that we've completed the sixth chapter, let's review some of the main tasks you learned:

- Determine when I2C is the best solution to drive hardware
- Create Python software to use the python-smbus module to drive an interface
- Drive servos via the I2C interface and the pitfalls and restrictions that apply to their use

In the next chapter, you will look at the design of a mobile Pi system, including power systems and remote access.

# 7
# Going Mobile with Raspberry Pi

In previous chapters, we viewed the Raspberry Pi as a desktop system with a connected display, keyboard, and mouse to simplify development tasks. Moving forward, you may have requirements where your Pi is required to run headless or mobile. To meet these new requirements, you need to reach across the network (wired or wireless) and perform tasks at the command line or even on the graphical desktop.

After completing this chapter, you will be able to:

- Create a command-line interface to the Raspberry Pi.
- Develop mobile power solutions for the Raspberry Pi.

## Remote access to the Raspberry Pi

Our primary focus is command-line access to a remote Pi. When connecting remotely, you can leave the graphical desktop in place so that it's there when you return to desktop operation. If you want to turn off the UI, which is not a design requirement—use the `raspi-config` command.

Even with the desktop interface turned off, it is still possible to access window-based applications. You just need to use **X11 remoting**.

To learn more, go to `http://elinux.org/RPi_Remote_Access`.

# Using PuTTY remote access

We will start by connecting from a PC to the Pi using **PuTTY** on Microsoft Windows.

PuTTY is an SSH (secure shell) client that can securely communicate with a remote SSH server. You may remember that the Pi has an SSH server; we enabled it in *Chapter 1, Getting Started with the Raspberry Pi*, during the configuration of the final installation.

You can check if SSH is enabled by using Task Manager. If it is enabled, you will see sshd running as a root task. If it is not running, perform the following steps:

1.  Open an LXterminal command prompt.
2.  Type sudo raspi-config and press *Enter*.
3.  Open the **Advanced** options.
4.  Enable the **SSH** option.
5.  Reboot the computer to enable SSH.

# Installing PuTTY on Microsoft Windows

Before you can install PuTTY, you need to download it from http://www.chiark. greenend.org.uk/~sgtatham/putty/download.html.

There is a single, standalone executable called putty.exe. Double-click on the file and the PuTTY client will start—no installation is required.

However, if you want documentation or some of the other optional functions, then download either putty.zip or putty-0.63-installer.exe. We advise that you download the installer file; it will place all the files in C:\Program Files\PuTTY by default and then create a Start Menu icon.

When you start **PuTTY**, you are presented with a configuration screen, as shown in the following screenshot:

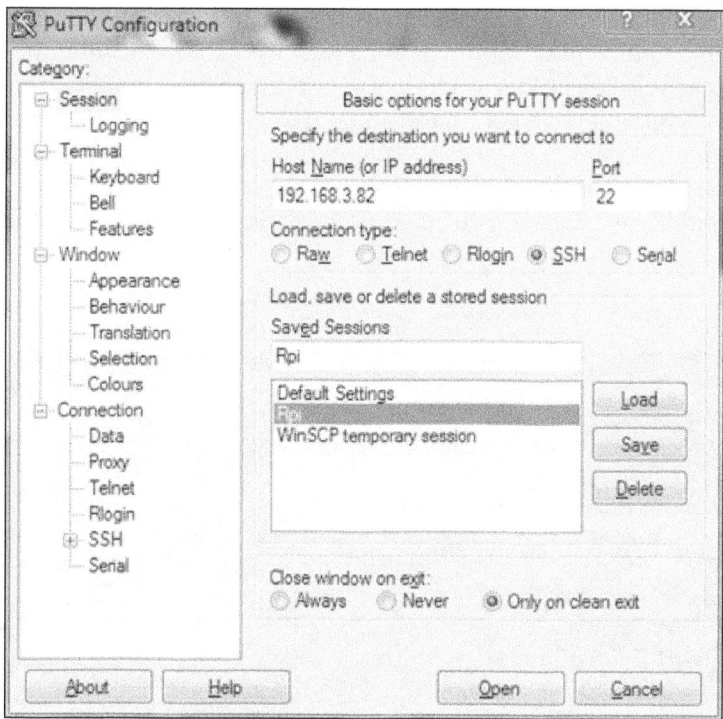

To complete the installation, refer to the following steps and the preceding screenshot showing the **PuTTY Configuration** screen:

1. Entered in the left-hand side window is the IP address of our Pi; you will need to enter the address of your Pi. To find the IP address, type `ip addr` at a command line and use the address given for `eth0` or `wlan0` depending on whether you have a wired or wireless connection.

2. Type a name for your **Saved Session** in the **Session** window. In the example shown, ours is called **Rpi**. Then, select **Save**.

3. Select **Open** to connect to your Pi as shown in the following screenshot. The first time you connect, you will get a pop-up window saying the RSA2 key is not cached. Select **Yes** to retain the key, and you won't be prompted again. Finally, you will get a command-line login prompt. You can use `pi` as the username and `raspberry` as the password (if you did not change it during the installation of the OS), as shown in the following screenshot. The command line opens at your user home directory, which in this case is `/home/pi`.

```
login as: pi
pi@192.168.3.82's password:
Linux raspberrypi 3.12.35+ #730 PREEMPT Fri Dec 19 18:31:24 GMT 2014 armv6l

The programs included with the Debian GNU/Linux system are free software;
the exact distribution terms for each program are described in the
individual files in /usr/share/doc/*/copyright.

Debian GNU/Linux comes with ABSOLUTELY NO WARRANTY, to the extent
permitted by applicable law.
Last login: Tue Jan  6 16:00:58 2015 from 192.168.3.104
pi@raspberrypi ~ $ pwd
/home/pi
pi@raspberrypi ~ $
```

The next time you open PuTTY, you can load the profile you filled out. The settings, including the IP address, are kept in this session profile.

# Remote access from Linux and OSX

Linux- and OSX-based systems have built-in SSH terminal utilities. Perform the following steps to get a command-line interface to the remote Pi:

1. Open a terminal window and enter `ssh pi@192.168.3.82` (make sure that you use your IP address in place of this one).

2. You'll be asked whether you want to continue the connection; select **Yes** to get a command-line interface to the remote Pi.

There are many utilities that can be used for remote access to the Raspberry Pi. One utility that can be purchased and is suitable for access from Linux, Windows, and Mac devices is **Remoter**, which you can purchase and download from `http://remoterlabs.com/`.

# Testing your remote session from a PC or Mac

If you still have your audio hooked up, you can use the Python text mode Internet radio application by performing the following steps.

1. From your command line, enter `cd radio/bin`.

2. Enter `python3 radio.py` to start the application.

The Internet radio should now play your selected station.

# Battery power systems

As we make the transition to a mobile system, we need to consider how the Pi will be powered. There are two kinds of batteries that are most relevant to our needs. First, there are primary batteries, such as the disposable, non-rechargeable style used in many appliances such as keyboards, mice, and torches. Second, there are the rechargeable kinds, such as those in a cellphone, a camera, or toys such as RC-cars that get used often.

The Raspberry Pi is not an ultra-low power device and is usually turned on for long periods of time, which makes rechargeable batteries the best solution. The most common rechargeable battery technologies are listed in the following table showing a performance comparison of various rechargeable batteries:

| Parameters | Ni-Cd | Ni-M-H | Liquid Li-ion | Polymer Li-ion |
|---|---|---|---|---|
| Voltage (V) | 1.2 | 1.2 | 3.6 | 3.6 |
| Weight energy density (Wh/Kg) | 50 | 80 | 125 | 170 |
| Volume energy density (Wh/l) | 150 | 200 | 320 | 400 |
| Cycle life (times) | 500 | 500 | 800 | 1000 |
| Self-discharge (%/month) | 25-30 | 30-35 | 6-9 | 2-5 |
| Electrolyte state | Liquid | Liquid | Liquid | Polymer Gel |

Note that the voltage shown in the table is a single-cell voltage, and battery packs may be made up of multiple cells, in series to increase the voltage, or in parallel to increase the current available.

# Selecting regulators

The Pi runs on a regulated 5V power supply. If the supply voltage goes below about 4.9V, the system may brown out. If the supply voltage goes over 5.25V, components may be damaged.

 There are no battery packs that provide 5V directly, so any power solutions need to have a regulator or power convertor of some type.

There are three commonly available regulator types in the hobby world:

1. **Linear regulator**: This regulator drops some of the battery pack voltage, so the pack voltage must always be above that required. This is the least efficient type of regulator since, to regulate it, it consumes considerable power compared to the output power required.

2. **Buck regulator**: Like the linear regulator, it drops the battery pack voltage to that required. However, as a switching regulator (power convertor), it is highly efficient (typically 85 percent or more).

3. **Boost regulator**: This regulator increases the battery voltage to that required. It's a switching regulator, so again typically it is highly efficient (typically 85 percent or more).

Let's look at a very simple power solution and make some observations about the regulator types.

For example, if we use 2 Li-ion batteries in series (2 x 3.6=7.2V) for the linear and buck regulators and 2 Li-ion batteries in parallel for the boost convertor (3.6 V), then we achieve the same battery energy storage value if the cells have identical ratings.

Referring to the following image, we will assume that we have a Raspberry Pi project that draws 1 Amp at 5V. So, as a math problem, we would write this as P = V x I, which is, 1 x 5 = 5 Watts. This is the dissipation of the Pi and does not include any losses in the regulators.

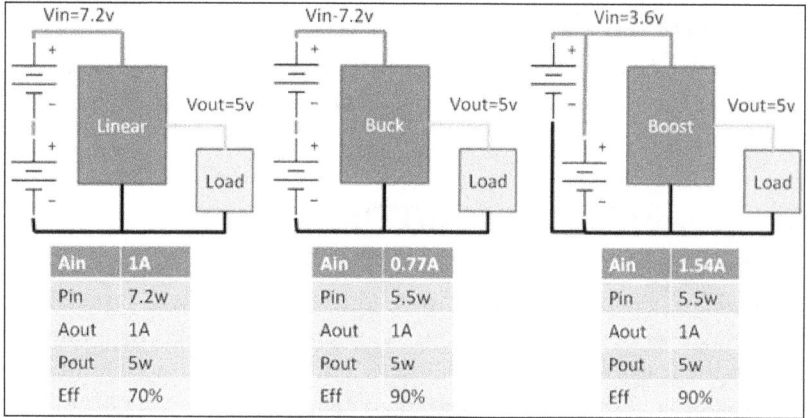

Note that in the preceding image, the **Buck convertor** draws less current (on average) than the load current required and the **Boost convertor** draws more current than the load. The linear regulator draws the same battery current as the output and has much greater losses. As you can see, the Buck/Boost solutions will have a longer battery life as they draw less power in total than the linear regulator.

 For those who would like to go more in depth for details about Buck and Boost convertors, the http://www.ti.com/lit/an/slva535a/slva535a.pdf TI Application report is a good starting point.

Based on the previous paragraph, it is clear that Buck and Boost convertors are more desirable where longer battery life is required. Moving forward, let's consider a couple of implementations that are viable for powering mobile Raspberry Pi projects. Both solutions will be Boost convertors.

# Measuring Raspberry Pi project current

To accurately measure the power consumed by a project can be challenging. Even if you own a multi-meter, you will still have the difficulty of how to break into the USB power line to measure current. To simplify this task, you can use a USB power monitor.

There are many types of power monitors available; some show just the voltage and current and some calculate the power consumed as well. We recommend the PortaPow USB Power Monitor V2 (http://www.portablepowersupplies.co.uk/portapow-usb-power-monitor-v2/).

# Potential battery power solutions

There are a huge number of options available to provide rechargeable battery solutions to power the Pi, but we will only consider a very small subset that is readily available.

## Adafruit PowerBoost 1000 Basic

This small boost convertor board uses a 3.6V Li-ion/Polymer battery to provide 5.2V on a standard USB-A connector. The chip used in this board will typically run at 95 percent efficiency. You decide what battery capacity is required for your project. The board shown in the following image has a low battery voltage indicator set at 3.2V, which is far down the battery discharge curve. Be prepared to recharge the battery as soon as the low-battery indicator light comes on. The following image shows the Adafruit PowerBoost 1000 Basic connected to a 3.7V Li-ion battery:

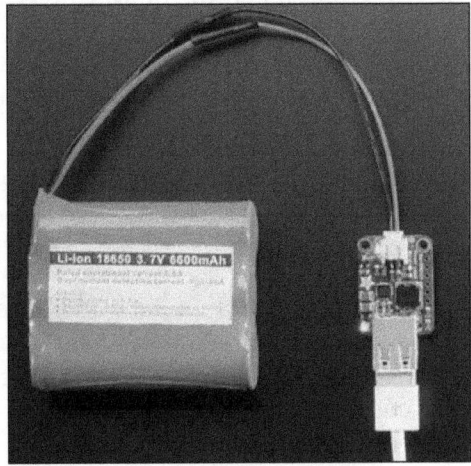

For example, if you have a Pi project that uses 500 mA of current rated at 5.2V (about 2.6 Watts), it will consume about 2.8 Watts in total. The battery approaches fully discharged at 3.6 V (about 4.2V when fully charged) and draws about 760 mA from the cell.

The batteries are specified in mA/hours, so the battery shown in the preceding image as 6600 mAh would most likely achieve 8 hours or more of battery life for the project (6600/760 = 8.6 hours).

To put this in real configuration terms, our Raspberry Pi with a PiCam camera, USB Wi-Fi adapter, and Sewell USB audio draws under 400 mA.

**Warning**: Do not use the same regulators to provide power to the Raspberry Pi and to heavy current peripherals such as DC motors. Always power this type of peripheral from separate power modules even if they use a common battery pack.

For more information, go to `http://www.adafruit.com/product/2030`,

# Adafruit PowerBoost 500C

Similar to the PowerBoost 1000, this small power convertor (`http://www.adafruit.com/product/1944`) can provide more than 500 mA of current rated at 5.2V and also includes a battery charger circuit. If you use a USB power supply capable of more than the current drawn from the battery by the project, then the battery will charge. The battery charge, however, is limited to 500 mA, so charge times may be quite long if you are using a significant portion of the output capability.

For example, if the current drawn from the battery is 400 mA, and the charger is limited to 500 mA, then effectively the battery charges at 100 mA or less.

You can consider this solution as almost a true **uninterrupted power supply (UPS)** for the Pi. It can be powered from the USB power supply until the power fails, and then it draws power from the battery pack. All it lacks is a means of telling the Pi that the power has failed. We think this might be an ideal power solution for small projects based on the new Pi Model A+.

If you are designing projects with the Pi and need a true UPS, there are solutions available. One example is the CW2 Pi UPS; for more information go to `http://piups.net/index.php`.

# Power banks as an alternative mobile power system

If you use a cellphone or tablet, you may already be aware of or are using a power bank to provide extra charging power when you travel. Power banks provide 5V at typically 1–2 Amps, with various power capacities. They are relatively inexpensive since they are produced in such high volumes.

One power bank that we tried with some success is the **Poweradd Pilot 2GS** (available from Amazon for about $22 at `http://www.amazon.com/Poweradd-Pilot-2GS-Technology-Blackberry/dp/B00ITILPZ4`. It has 10000 mAh of Li-Polymer battery. You can plug in to a USB charger, which powers the project and charges the battery at the same time.

Be aware that there is an architecture problem with the charging circuit for most power banks, including the Poweradd Pilot 2GS. If you plug in or unplug the USB charger, the output is momentarily turned off, which automatically resets your Pi. So, you would not consider this solution a viable UPS. The following image shows a Poweradd Pilot 2GS disassembled:

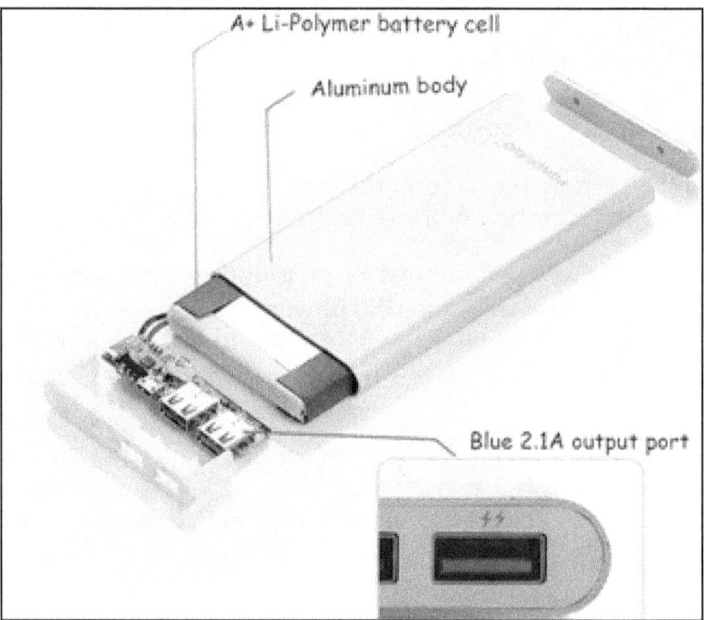

# Project 1 – Selecting a project battery capacity

In our next chapter, we will begin building a robot line follower, and we know the Pi will need to be mobile and battery powered for this. Let's define what needs to be powered and just how big (mAh) our battery needs to be. First, let's lay out the specifications:

- Raspberry Pi B+, Wi-Fi adapter, PiCam, Adafruit 16-Channel I2C servo board (servo power is separate) powered by a single battery pack
- Run time of at least 1 hour on an Adafruit PowerBoost 1000

While your Pi is still a desktop system, perform the following steps:

1. Configure the Wi-Fi adapter (you have a wireless network connection with a fixed IP address when Ethernet is disconnected).
2. Use the `raspi-config` command to turn off the LXDE/Openbox desktop, and then perform a shutdown.
3. Disconnect the power supply and all peripheral devices except those mentioned in the specifications.
4. Connect a USB power monitor and reconnect the power to the Pi.
5. The Pi Power LED should come on, the drive-access LED will flash, the PWM power LED should be on and, within a minute or so, the Wi-Fi adapter access LED should begin to flash.
6. Record the current on the USB power monitor. On our system, the current was approximately 330 mA for a Raspberry Pi model B+.
7. Connect from your PC or Mac to the Raspberry Pi using SSH and verify that your connection works using simple command-line access.
8. Shut down the system using the `sudo shutdown -h now` command, and then reconnect as a desktop system.

The AdaFruit PowerBoost 1000 uses a single-cell Li-Po/Li-Ion battery. The battery current will be higher than what the Raspberry Pi consumes because it is a Boost regulator. The regulator is also set to a slightly higher output voltage, 5.2V, and we'll have to take this into account when working out the power and current drawn from the battery. In our case, the power consumed by the Pi is: $P = V \times A$, $0.33 \times 5.2 = 1.7$ Watts. With a convertor efficiency of approximately 90 percent, this would mean about 1.9 Watts consumed from the battery. The battery-low voltage is 3.6V and, at this voltage, the battery current would be $1.9/3.6 = 528$ mA.

AdaFruit offers a Li-Polymer 3.7V 500 mAh battery (Product 1578) for $8, which is not enough to meet our 1-hour runtime target. They also offer a Li-Polymer 3.7V 1200 mAh (Product 258) for $10, and a Li-Polymer 3.7 V 2500 mAh (Product 328) for $15.

It looks like the 1200 mAh battery connected to an AdaFruit PowerBoost 1000 would meet the needs of our project and most likely provide over 1 hour of runtime. The battery capacity reduces as batteries get older and/or if they are cold so, in most cases, it is wise to use a larger capacity provided weight is not a problem. Your results may be a little different to ours depending on the USB Wi-Fi adapter you use, the model of the PiCam camera, and, of course, the batteries available to you.

Once you have selected and procured your battery and regulator/convertor, you should test the operation and runtime. If the regulator/convertor you choose does not have a clear indication of battery charge level (or voltage), then plan to be conservative in your use of the runtime. It may be better to have two batteries and only use 50–70 percent of the runtime capability before recharging.

# Summary

Now that we've completed the seventh chapter, let's review some of the main tasks you learned:

- Connecting to a Raspberry Pi remotely using SSH
- Determining the regulator/convertor type most appropriate for your project
- Determining the appropriate battery capacity to power a Raspberry Pi project

In the next chapter we will design a line-following robot, but instead of using IR sensors, we will use the PiCam camera.

# 8
# Creating a Raspberry Pi Line-following Robot

In *Chapter 7, Going Mobile with the Raspberry Pi*, we covered most of what was required to go mobile with our Raspberry Pi. In this final chapter, we will bring together all of the hardware and software needs and show what is required to work with a mobile application or, more specifically, with a line-following robot. As usual, we will try to stay at the desktop till the last possible moment before disconnecting all of our peripherals, such as the keyboard, mouse, and display.

After completing this chapter, you will be able to:

- Create applications that communicate over pipes to implement a message-driven robot interface
- Design a methodology to implement a line-following robot, including start/stop and shutdown buttons
- Design a text-based remote interface to control a robot
- Design a physical robot with a mobile Raspberry Pi controller

## Implementing a line-following robot

Robot line followers come in all shapes, sizes, and speeds. From very simple devices, with just a few transistors, to microcomputer-controlled versions, the basic strategy is still the same—follow a marked line on a floor.

The Raspberry Pi, with its powerful operating system, might seem like overkill for the task at hand. However, you can learn a great deal from designing and developing applications(s) and hardware and working through potential limitations.

The majority of line-following robot designs use **infrared** (**IR**) sensors or **light-dependent resistors** (**LDR**)) to sense the reflectivity of tape when it is used as the line to follow. These sensors invariably require A/D (analog to digital) convertors or amplifiers and level detectors to sense the target tape. When using a small microcomputer to drive a robot, you may have the required A/D and level-sensing hardware built in, and it may be capable of capturing a thousand or so samples per second.

In the case of the Pi, we do not have an analog hardware interface available. We could, of course, connect an I2C A/D converter; you can view one example of this type at `http://www.adafruit.com/product/1085` which uses a 4 channel `ADS1115`. The 16 bit A/D chip is capable of capturing about 800 samples per second, so if you had 4 IR sensors, you could potentially capture readings from the field of view at about 200 samples per second (it's quite another question whether or not you actually need to sample at such a high data rate).

For this project, we will use our PiCam to capture a view of the tape we follow. Using a camera creates some interesting software challenges, but they are fun to try and solve. We know based on our projects completed in previous chapters that the PiCam can capture video clips (frames) at a high rate (30–60 fps). We also know that high video frame rates are a real challenge once you have to acquire and then analyze single frames, as we did with the security system in *Chapter 3, Raspberry Pi and Cameras*. When you have to analyze frames, the frame rates drop dramatically, and achieving even 10 fps on the Pi is challenging.

If you have no previous experience in robotics, we recommend that you do a little research online; a good place to start is `http://www.seattlerobotics.org/encoder/200011/LineDetect2.htm`.

# Line-following robot architecture

Our architecture for a line-following robot will have a specific set of features, which are:

- Wireless remote access to the robot
- Text-driven interface for remote control using Python
- Buttons on the robot to start/stop and shutdown the robot processing
- A single PiCam camera sensor
- Two-wheel drive with a dragging tail

We will provide you with a downloadable-parts list for this model, but, you could just as easily implement it as either a tracked or four-wheel skid-steer robot. The following image is our line-following robot:

# Software architecture

We will develop our robot based on a multi-module approach. This strategy will enable you to analyze the methodology used to implement the robot. The software architecture for our line-following robot is shown in the following image:

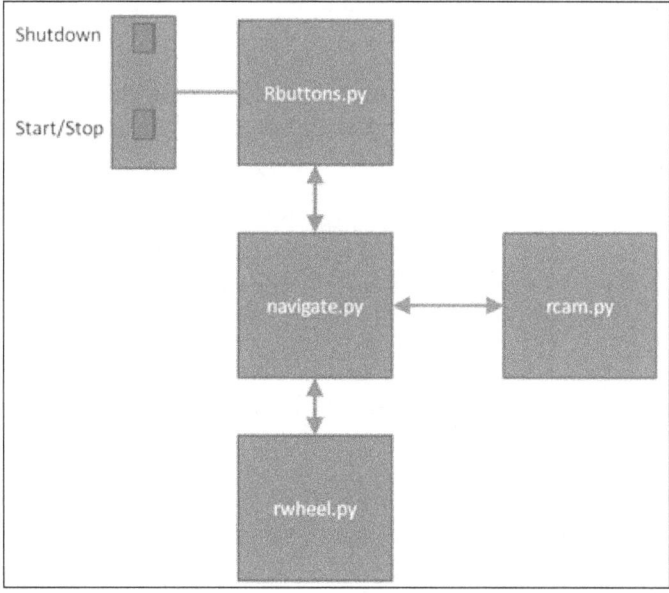

# Software module functions

Each software module in the architecture will have a specific function, as detailed in the following table:

| Module | Description |
|--------|-------------|
| navigate.py | When started, this module starts the rbuttons.py, rcam.py, and rwheel.py applications. This module queries the rcam.py module for camera data, and based on that information, sets the speed of the two wheels via the rwheel.py module. |
| rbuttons.py | This monitors the buttons on the robot using the GPIO library. It returns the status of the buttons or sets the LEDs on and off based on requests from rnavigate.py. |
| rcam.py | This reads a single frame from the PiCam, processes each line in the frame, and returns the derived data to the navigate module. |
| rwheel.py | This accepts the wheel speed command from the navigate module and sets the servo speeds over the I2C PWM board. |

All the modules are separate command-line-driven Python programs so that you can run each one in isolation to debug and test. When they are used to control the robot, they communicate over pipes connected to the **stdin** and **stdout** ports for each of the applications.

We could implement these modules as a single multithreaded application, but, this would require unnecessarily complex code development. We intentionally used pipes between the separate applications, making the software easier to understand and modify.

Our project plan is to do all the development using the desktop, as we have done in earlier chapters, and to use a mobile and remote configuration only when we have everything working.

To learn how to create routines that interpret user input commands and instantiate the programs that navigate.py needs to talk to, go to the Chapter 8 folder at http://1drv.ms/1ysAxkl or the code bundle for this book, and download and read the *Chapter 8a, Interpreting Commands and Testing Modules* file before proceeding to the next topic.

You can download all the Python programs for the robot project from http://1drv.ms/1ysAxkl.

You will notice that the program files are in the /robot directory. Create a directory /home/pi/robot or copy the directory from your downloaded files.

# Implementing rbuttons.py

The first module we will analyze is the rbuttons.py file; it uses the RPi.GPIO library to enable an LED to be driven and uses two switches to be sensed. If you remember, back in *Chapter 5, Port Input and Output on the Raspberry Pi*, we told you that the use of the GPIO library functions requires root privileges. At that time, we suggested starting the Python 2 IDLE IDE using the command line sudo idle to get the required root privileges. This got around the problem of development, and again here, you can start IDLE from the command line. We will programmatically set the required privileges when we eventually run all the programs together.

# Downloading rbuttons.py and test-buttons.py

If you have a non-root privilege instance of IDLE open now, close it and perform the following steps from the command line:

1. Open a new instance of the Python IDE using the sudo idle command.

2. Download rbuttons.py and test-buttons.py from the Chapter 8 folder at http://1drv.ms/1ysAxkl into your /home/pi/robot directory.

3. Open rbuttons.py in the Python IDE.

4. Review the key functions as follows:

    ° main(): This code calls the initgpio() function, listens for input on the stdin port, handles most errors, and sends the ok: output to stdout. It also has the Popen() function that sets up the commands to be recognized.

> Notice in the following code fragment that there are three whitelisted commands — LEDon, LEDoff, and rdswevents — that can be responded to. If you still have the LED and switches set up from *Chapter 5, Port Input and Output on the Raspberry Pi*, you could use them again for this test. The software handles four switches even though we will only implement two in the robot. We used GPIO26 for the LED, and GPIO21 and GPIO20 for the two switches. We implemented this schematic on a small prototyping area on the PWM controller for our robot.

Following the schematic shown after the following code, you will add the switches and the LED to achieve the same functionality. The schematic for the LED and switches is shown after the following code and shows the ports for the LED and switches:

```
cmddata = eval(inputstr,{'__builtins__':None},
                 {'LEDon':LEDon,
                  'LEDoff':LEDoff,
                  'rdswevents':rdswevents })
```

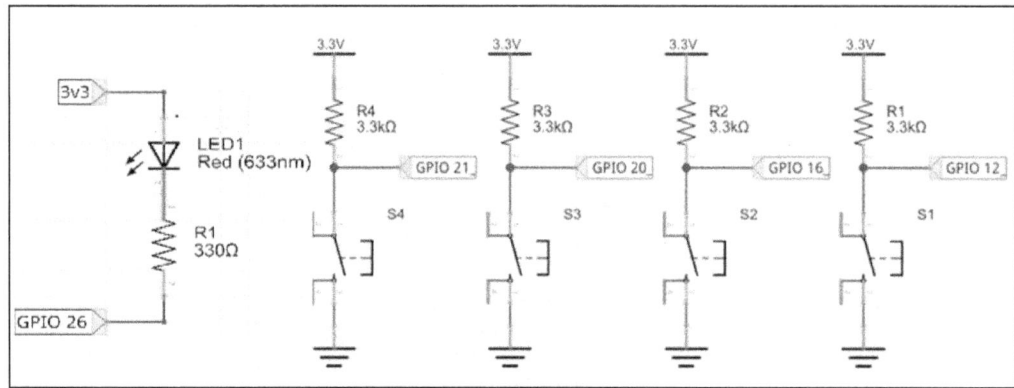

- ○   `initgpio()`: This is identical to the code we used in *Chapter 5, Port Input and Output on the Raspberry Pi*. It sets up the various GPIO ports and adds an event detector to monitor each of the switches. The detection occurs on a separate thread that allows polling of the port activity indicator.

- ○   `LEDon()` and `LEDoff()`: These two functions set and clear, respectively, the digital I/O pin to drive the LED.

- ○   `Rdswevents()`: This uses a `for` loop to iterate through the event flags and builds a list with the status for each.

In the following code fragment, the `for` loop iterates through a tuple containing the switch ports (21, 20, 16, 12), reading the event flag for each switch. When the event detector registers the status change, it will hold it until the flag is read. When the flag is read, it is also reset, so the event detector is ready for the next event. Here's the aforementioned code fragment:

```
def rdswevents():
  swevents=[]
  for i in (switchports):
    if GPIO.event_detected(i):
        swevents.append(1)
```

```
else:
    swevents.append(0)
flushout (str(swevents) + ' ' )
```

If you run the program within the Python IDE, the console output will look like this:

```
ok:
LEDon
ok:
LEDoff
ok:
rdswevents
[0, 0, 0, 0] ok:
```

 Note the string output for `rdswevents`; you can build back into a `list []` quite easily.

5. Familiarize yourself with the code in `rbuttons.py`.

6. Close the root privileged instance of Idle.

7. To test `rbuttons.py`, go to the `Chapter 8` folder at `http://1drv.ms/1ysAxk1`, and in the `Chapter 8A` supplemental materials folder, read `Testing rbuttons.py` to run `test-buttons.py`.

# Implementing rcam.py

The second module we will explore is `rcam.py`; it uses the PiCam and **Python Image Library** (PIL, which is part of Pillow) to capture frames from the PiCam and return processed data from the image. The processing overhead for camera images is very CPU intensive. Using advanced library functions such as **OpenCV**, you might find it challenging to capture more than one or two frames per second on the Pi. Our camera would need to capture at least 5 frames per second (a snapshot of the line every 200 ms) if we expect the robot to move more than 2 inches per second.

To allow the best possible performance for our implementation, we plan to:

1.  Minimize the frame size to reduce the amount of data we need to process. We will chose a frame size of 100 x 20 pixels and set the camera to capture frames at 60 fps (we won't capture frames at this rate, but it sets the camera speed to acquire an image). The camera is positioned on the robot at about 2–2.5 inches above the floor. The 100 x 20 pixels provides about 3.5 inches of horizontal **field of view** (**FOV**) and about 0.7 inches of vertical FOV on the floor.

2.  Capture frame data into a memory-resident array to speed up the transfer from the camera to the image plane for analysis.

3.  Process data minimally, looking mainly for adjacent runs of black (or very dark) pixels in each scanline to identify the line. Since the PiCam is a color camera, we will choose to look for the line color rather than a brightness- or contrast-based detection value.

A raw image of a test line (no sharpening or filters applied) in the 100 x 20 format from the camera is shown as follows:

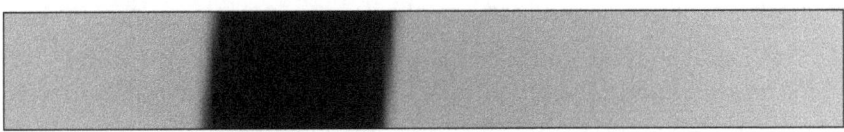

We used a 0.75-inch black electrical insulation tape on a cream-colored background with only ambient lighting.

# Installing the pip manager

We won't use the `apt-get` command string to install the **PIL**. Instead, we will install another package manager called **pip** that knows how to locate and install the PIL. The pip installer is used to install Python-specific packages, and in this case, we will install a branch of the PIL called **Pillow**.

## Installing the pip package manager

To install the pip package manager, from the command line, type `sudo apt-get install pip`.

You can read the documentation for pip at `https://pip.pypa.io/en/latest/user_guide.html`.

# Installing Pillow

Before installing Pillow, there are prerequisite libraries and tools that must be installed. Since the prerequisite-file list is quite long, we have created a Bash script to ease the installation task. Download the `load-pillow` script file from the `Chapter 8` folder at `http://1drv.ms/1ysAxkl` into your `/home/pi/robot` directory. Open a Terminal command line in the `/home/pi/robot` directory and complete the following command steps:

1. `sudo apt-get update`
2. `sudo apt-get upgrade`
3. `chmod +x load-pillow`
4. `sudo ./load-pillow`

The scripted install should end with a success message for the Pillow installation. If this does not occur, then copy and execute the individual command lines in the **load-pillow** script and ensure each one succeeds.

# Downloading rcam.py

Download `rcam.py` from the `Chapter 8` folder at `http://1drv.ms/1ysAxkl` to the `/home/pi/robot` directory and open an instance of the Python 2 IDE. We do not need a root-privileged instance of IDLE for the camera to work.

Review the key functions of `rcam.py` in the following table:

| Function | Description |
|---|---|
| `main()` | This calls `initcam(camwidth,camheight,camfps)` and then listens for input on the `stdin` port, handles most errors, and sends the `ok:` output to `stdout`. It also has the `Popen()` function that sets up the commands to be recognized. |
| | `cmddata = eval(inputstr,{'__builtins__':None},` `{'line0':line0,` `'line18':line18,` `'line018':line018,` `'close':closecam })` |
| | Note that in the code fragment, there are four whitelisted commands recognized. The commands `line0`, and `line18` return data for the respective line number. The command `line018` returns data for both `line 0` and `line 18` `close` exits the application and exits the application. |
| `initcam()` | This sets up the camera and the in-memory capture stream. |
| `acquire()` | This sets up the image array and does the line processing. |

If you run the program within the Python IDE, the console output will look like this:

```
ok:
line0
(207, 24, 24, 66, 1308, 58), ok:
line18
(134, 25, 25, 66, 1350, 57), ok:
line018
(205, 24, 24, 66, 1308, 58), (131, 25, 25, 66, 1350, 57), ok:
```

 Notice the string output of line values, which can be built back into a list [] quite easily.

1. Familiarize yourself with the code in the IDE.

2. Close rcam.py.

3. To test rcam.py, go to the Chapter 8 folder at http://1drv.ms/1ysAxkl, and in the Chapter 8 Supplemental Materials folder, open the *Interpreting Commands and Testing Modules* document to read the *Test rcam.py* section.

# Implementing rwheel.py

The third module we will explore is rwheel.py; it uses the smbus library to access I2C peripherals. If you remember, back in *Chapter 6, Driving I2C Peripherals on the Raspberry Pi*, the use of the smbus library functions requires root privileges and is limited to Python 2. At that time, we suggested starting the Python 2 IDLE IDE using the sudo idle command line. This strategy resolved a potential development problem, so again, you should start IDLE from the command line. We will programmatically set the required privileges when we use all the programs together.

## Downloading rwheel.py and test-rwheel.py

To download rwheel.py and test-rwheel.py files, perform the following steps:

1. Use the command line to open a new instance using sudo idle.

2. Download the rwheel.py and test-rwheel.py from the Chapter 8 folder at http://1drv.ms/1ysAxkl.

3. Open rwheel.py in the Python IDE.

4. Review the key functions in the following table:

| Function | Description |
|---|---|
| main() | This function calls the PCA9685_reset(), setPWMFreq() and servonuetral() functions to initialize the AdaFruit 16-Channel PWM and then listens for command input on stdin, handles most errors, and sends the ok: output to the stdout port. It also has the eval() function that sets up the commands to be recognized. Here's the code for this function:<br><br>`cmddata = eval(inputstr,{'__builtins__':None},`<br>`                {'servonuetral':servonuetral,`<br>`                'servowr':servowr,`<br>`                    'servord':serord,`<br>`                    'close':closeandexit`<br>`})`<br><br>Note that in the code fragment, there are four whitelisted commands recognized — servonuetral, servowr, servord, and close — that can be responded to. Note also that the close command is remapped to the Closeandexit function. |
| servord() | This function reads from a PWM channel. To use this, you enter a comma-separated value using the syntax servord, chan#. The chan# syntax can be 0-15, and there is no range checking in the function. The function returns a comma delimited string, such as 370, ok:. |
| servowr() | This function writes to a PWM channel. To use this, you enter comma-separated values using the syntax servowr, chan#, Value#. The chan# can be 0-15, and the Value# can be 0-4095. In this application using RC servos, the neutral value is approximately 370, and there is no error-checking of the value range.<br><br>Note that the low level definitions that read/write to the I2C bus are unchanged from that used in *Chapter 6, Driving I2CPeripherals on the Raspberry Pi*, with the exception that error print statements are changed to use the flushout() function. |

If you run the program within the Python IDE, the console output will look similar to this:

```
ok:
servowr, 5, 400
ok:
servord, 5
ok:
400, ok:
Servonuetral
ok:
```

5. Close the root-privileged instance of IDLE.

6. To test rwheel.py, go to the Chapter 8 folder at http://1drv.ms/1ysAxkl and into the Chapter 8 Supplemental Materials folder to read the *Testing rwheel.py* section.

# Implementing navigate.py

The final module for our line-following robot is navigate.py. This program initiates the pipes that will instantiate the rbuttons.py, rcam.py, and rwheel.py programs as separate processes using multiple Popen() functions. It provides a minimal user-text-mode interface, provides the logic to handle button functions, and most importantly provides the logic to steer the robot.

# Downloading navigate.py

The following shows the steps to download navigate.py as well as the explanation of the code's functionality:

1. Use the command line to open a new instance of the Python 2 IDLE (it does not need to have root privilege).

2. Download navigate.py from the Chapter 8 folder at http://1drv.ms/1ysAxkl

3. Open navigate.py in the Python IDE (non-privileged).

4. Review the main() function as follows:

```
def main():
    if startpipes():
        print 'Aborting....something did not start!'
        sys.exit('Closing application')
    #Start scanning loop
    while True :
        try:
            start=time()
            #Button and LED commands
            sensebuttons()
            flashLED()
            if paused :
                print ' Paused....                \r',
                setwheel(leftwheel, neutral)
                setwheel(rightwheel, neutral)
                sleep(0.04)
```

```
        else:
            #Camera commands
            readcamera()
            #Wheel commands
            setLRspeed()
            #Calculate loop time
            stop=time()
            print ' Loop = ', str(round((1 / (stop-
            start)), 2)), '\r',
    except KeyboardInterrupt :
        break
    #Tidy up before we leave
    tidyexit()


if __name__ == '__main__':

    main()
```

 Note that in the preceding listing, the main() function is primarily an infinite loop writing and reading the pipes to our processes, and the only way out of the program is to hit *Ctrl + C*.

As you read the code, pay particular attention to the following key elements:

- When started, the program initiates the pipes using startpipes(); if there is an instantiation error, we simply exit.

- The while True loop reads the time used to calculate our loop frequency and then communicates with each of the external applications to drive the robot. This is a very simple serial scheduler, and it blocks on each readline() from the external processes. The service loop consists of the following functions, as shown in the following table:

| Function | Description |
|---|---|
| sensebuttons() | This routine looks for button activity on GPIO(21), which will shutdown the computer, and GPIO(20), which will toggle the pause state. You will remember from earlier testing that each transaction with rbuttons.py costs about 1.25 ms. |
| flashLED () | This routine uses the same GPIO functions and either turns on or off the status LED. If the robot is paused, the LED flashes at half the loop time. The time varies between a slow flash if the camera is being used, and a fast flash if the robot is paused. |

| Function | Description |
|---|---|
| readcamera() | This routine reads line0 from rcam.py and, based on the return values, sets the parameters to program wheel speeds. |
| setLRspeed() | This routine writes the required servowr, x, y parameters for rwheel.py to configure the servos on channels 0 and 1 of the I2C PWM board to provide robot motion. |

At the end of the while loop (if the camera and wheels were accessed) the stop time is read and the loop time as a frequency is calculated and printed. If the robot is not paused, the loop time is dominated by the time taken to capture and provide frame data. The mathematical formula is 1/(stop-start) and varies in the range of 5–8 frames per second. If the robot is paused, then the loop time is not calculated but is dominated by the 40-ms sleep timer (which is only used when paused). The LED will therefore flash at about 2.5–4 Hz when not paused and about 12 Hz when paused.

# The steering methodology

There are many techniques used to provide steering control for wheeled and tracked robots; some are complex mathematically and require closed-loop control, and some do not. Here, we have implemented a simple fuzzy-logic control that is easy to understand and does not require closed-loop wheel-speed detection or a software PID controller.

To understand the simple algorithm used, we need to understand the data based on which steering and speed decisions will be made. We also need to understand where errors may occur and allow for them.

# Open loop servo control

When you set a particular speed for the wheel servos on the robot, what speed will the robot travel at? The fact is that we don't actually know. The servo wheel drive is described as open loop; there are no wheel sensors to provide verification that the wheel is even turning. There could also be many small variations in servo speed due to the supply voltage, the calibration of each servo, the diameter of the wheels, and even the gear ratios within the servo that might differ by some small amount.

If we set the forward speed of the robot to a number (say 400 on the left wheel and 340 on the right wheel), you'd expect that the robot would move in a straight line. It won't. It will veer slightly to the left or right, perhaps not by much, but there will be an error. You can check this out using `rwheels.py` to chart the error on your own robot.

Here, we will ignore all the variations in the wheel speed that might occur and just watch for variation in where the line is in the camera view.

# Analyzing camera data

When the `navigate.py` software requests `line0` from `rcam.py`, we need to discuss the data that is returned. The string returned is of the form `(207, 24, 24, 66, 1308, 58)`, `ok:`. As shown in the following table, there are six values returned; let's deal with them as a tuple, `X=(207, 24, 24, 66, 1308, 58)`, to discuss the meaning of each:

| Value | Description |
|---|---|
| X[0] | This is the average of the sum of all RGB pixel values that were classified as black in `line0`. Since black has very small individual R,G, and B values (we set the individual values at less than 25 in a 255 range), this number should be reasonably small. |
| X[1] | The total number of pixels in `line0` is classified as black. |
| X[2] | The largest number of adjacent pixels in `line0` is classified as black. This should be the line we want to follow, and as illustrated in the values used, the total black X[1] and X[2] are equal, so there are no black noise pixels. So, we have a clear picture of the line. |
| X[3] | This is the far-right column number of the largest set of adjacent black pixels. This is the right-hand side edge of the tape. Knowing the width of the tape (X[2]), we could calculate the column value for the center of the tape. |
| X[4] | This is the sum of the column numbers (0-100) for all black pixels. Provided X[1] and X[2] are equal, this represents a value that shows the line position from left to right. |
| X[5] | This is the number representing the error position on the left or right of the values represented by X[1]. This value is initialized to 50, and if the pixels are <50, they decrement this value; if they are >50, they increment the value. Providing X[1] and X[2] are equal, this error value can be used to steer the robot back toward an ideal condition where there are an equal number of pixels to the left and right of the center. |

The steering logic uses only one of the values shown in the preceding table (X[5], the left/right error number). The images captured using our robot were noise-free (X[1]=X[2]) all the time), so we even left out the equality check. The error number has a value range of about 26–74, with the black tape having an X[2] width of about 23–25 when normal to the line of the tape. If the robot is at an angle to the tape, then the target looks wider, the range increases, and the error value increases rapidly as the robot moves forward, as shown in the following diagram:

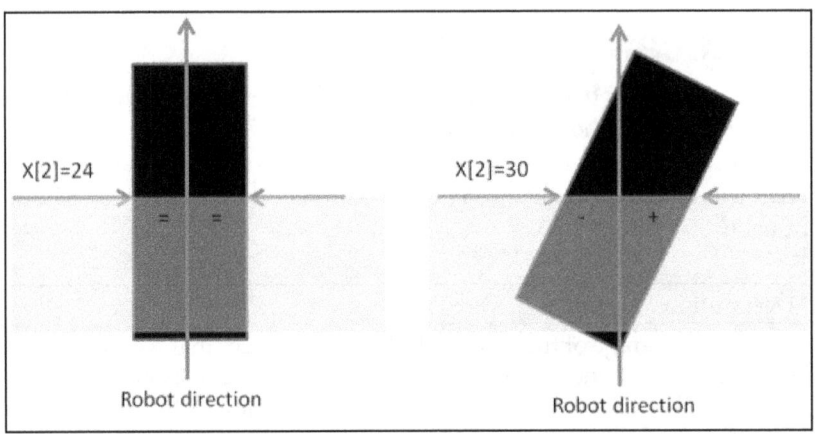

## Steering algorithm

The fuzzy logic has only three settings in the readcamera() function in navigate. py program:

| Deadzone | If the error value is >= 47 and <=52 | No steering, and increase **basespeed** by 1 each time through the loop, with a maximum base speed at 40 |
|----------|--------------------------------------|--------------------------------------------------------------------------------------------------------|
| **Stage 1 error** | If error value is >= 40 and <= 60 | Steer left or right by 6 to reduce errors and set the basespeed to15 |
| **Stage 2 error** | If error value is <= 40 and >= 60 | Steer left or right by 9 to reduce errors and set the basespeed at 10 |

Each time through the steering loop, only one of the three tests will execute. While there are particular numbers set here for the base speed and **steer speed**, we have no real knowledge of what the values mean. We could have just as easily described the speed as *slow*, *fast*, and *really fast*. In the same way, the steer value could be *Don't skew*, *Skew gently*, and *Skew hard* since they simply set a differential value added to the speed of each servo. The only value we could actually depend on is X[5] since this tells us where the line is within the camera field of view, and even that is fuzzy since it changes with the angle at which we view the tape.

# Time to build the mobile system

We are just about finished with the software development on the desktop, and the next phase is to check out the Wi-Fi configuration and build the Pi into a mobile system that is positioned on the robot. We used an 8 ½"x 4" x ½" plastic tray to hold the battery pack, camera, and the Pi. We then mounted it on the robot chassis using four pillars that positioned the camera about 2" off the ground. You can look at the detailed images of our robot in the download items for this chapter at http://1drv.ms/1ysAxkl and use the same parts list or design your own platform.

# Checking wireless connectivity

Before we shift from our desktop system to a mobile system, we need to make sure that the wireless configuration will connect automatically. When using the desktop, we had a utility that kept us connected to the right network. But now that we are about to turn off the desktop, we need to check that the low-level configuration will connect up when we need it to.

Using a root-privileged instance of File Manager, open /etc/network/interfaces. The file should look like this:

```
auto lo
iface lo inet loopback
iface eth0 inet dhcp
allow-hotplug wlan0
iface wlan0 inet dhcp
wpa-conf /etc/wpa_supplicant/wpa_supplicant.conf
iface default inet dhcp
```

If the configuration information for `wlan0` does not exist or differs from the preceding configuration, add it and then save the file.

Once you have checked the interfaces file, open the `/etc/wpa_supplicant/wpa_supplicant.conf` file.

The contents should look like this:

```
ctrl_interface=DIR=/var/run/wpa_supplicant GROUP=netdev
update_config=1
network={
ssid="ADDYOURSSID"
psk="ADDYOURPASSWORD"
}
```

If the configuration information for your Wi-Fi network does not exist in the file, add it and then save the file.

Unplug your Ethernet cable, ensure your USB wireless adapter is plugged into one of the motherboard USB sockets and open an LXterminal command window:

1. Type `sudo ifdown wlan0`.
2. Type `sudo ifup wlan0`.

You should see on the last line of the text output something similar to `bound to 192.1168.3.82` (your IP address will be different). This information tells you that the Raspberry Pi is connected to your Wi-Fi network.

Next, from the command window, start the `raspi-config` utility using the command `sudo raspi-config` and set the **Enable Boot to Desktop** option to **Console Text Console**. Exit `raspi-config` and accept the reboot option.

When the Pi reboots, it will be at a console login screen . You can log in locally or connect from a remote computer. If you have difficulties with remote connections or the Wi-Fi, you can check the *Remote access to the Raspberry Pi* section in *Chapter 7, Going Mobile with Raspberry Pi*, or the *Hardware and software networking configuration* section in *Chapter 2, Configuring the Raspberry Pi Desktop and Software*, for help.

If you need to get back to your desktop development environment, you can type `startx` in the command line. This is where the value of having most of your USB peripherals connected via a hub becomes important. You only need to plug in your monitor and hub to get back to desktop development. Then, reboot your system to return to the console login.

# Line-following robot

In the following image, you can see that the I2C PWM card is mounted externally on the Pi case due to a lack of holes in the case to allow for the servo leads:

Note the following assembly details in the preceding image:

- We used the Poweradd Pilot 2GS USB Powerbank to power the system which gave a ridiculously long runtime of about 12 hours for the Raspberry Pi alone, but increased the weight considerably.
- The servo power is from a 4 x AA size battery holder mounted onto the frame.
- The camera is mounted through a hole in the tray with two foam washers allowing easy extraction from the robot.
- The shutdown and start/pause switches and LED are wired into a small breadboard area on the I2C board.

# Assembling the robot

We assembled our robot from readily available parts that are available from multiple sources and in most countries.

If you decide to use a robot kit, select one with a tail dragger or skid steer configuration based on a two-wheel drive. Keep in mind that our design is not suitable for a robot configuration using Ackerman steering.

The base framework for our robot was built using **Actobotic** parts that are readily available in the US, Canada, UK, and France, although the links we use are to http://www.ServoCity.com in the U.S. We used a food container lid as the base on which to mount the Raspberry Pi and Power Bank. A flat plastic plate would suit just as well.

The base robot looks like this:

If you want to build a robot based on our parts list, the previous image should provide enough details for the assembly. Use the following guidelines:

- The DU-BRO tail wheel assembly needs a 0.125" hole drilled in one end if secured by two screws. Two 0.5" 6-32 screws and **Nylock** nuts secure it to the channel.

- The two small battery holder clamps visible at the bottom of the channel hold the 4 x AA battery pack in place inside the channel. We eventually connected the servo power to Powerbank after checking that it was able to supply the current requirements without problems.

- The canister lid we used has two 0.5" holes drilled in it. One allows the cables from the servo and the battery pack up to the tray, the other (1.5" forward of the servo axle) allows the PiCam to be held in position. We used some IC antistatic pad foam cut into two washers to hold the camera.

We used small adhesive Velcro stripes to hold the Powerbank in place in the tray. On top of the Powerbank, a further two strips help the Raspberry Pi in place.

The Raspberry Pi case we used was supplied as part of the Canakit for the Raspberry Pi B+. You need to select a case suitable for your Raspberry Pi model.

You can go to the Chapter 8 folder on http://1drv.ms/1ysAxkl and download the parts list called Robot_Parts.docx.

# How to bring up your robot

You will need to bring up your robot in an orderly fashion, testing each module and its associated hardware. Using a step-by-step procedure will give you important information about how the robot is working and help to resolve bugs.

First, place your robot on a small box or book that holds the wheels off the ground by about 0.5" and then connect your display, keyboard, and mouse.

Second, test your camera with a small preview window or by capturing an image. You can then adjust focus (our camera had this adjustment). Use a small piece of black tape on a white sheet of paper as a target. You can move this back and forth to measure your field of view.

Third, test your wheel drive and ensure that you have the servos connected to the correct PWM ports.

Finally, test the pause/start and shutdown buttons. The buttons are not essential, and you might elect to start and stop via a remote connection instead. We found that the buttons were very useful when the robot was in motion. Finally, you can run the navigate.py program and use a target, as mentioned earlier, to move the camera and test whether or not the robot is actually following the line.

# Navigating the robot

From your remote console connection, you can log in to the Pi and start the navigate application or run any of the individual applications to check your assembly and configuration on the floor layout. You can also set the navigate.py application to start at reboot (the applications starts in the paused condition) and use the start/pause and shutdown buttons to control the robot.

# Summary

Now that we've completed the final chapter, let's review some of the main tasks you learned how to do:

- Create applications that communicate over pipes to implement a message-driven robot interface
- Design a methodology to implement a line-following robot, including the start/stop and shutdown buttons
- Implement a text-based local or remote command-line interface to control a robot
- Design a physical robot with a mobile Raspberry Pi controller

Congratulations! You have completed our *Raspberry Pi Essentials* book.

While exploring complex software and hardware concepts, you discovered that the Pi is an amazing little computer. Working through several challenging projects, you incrementally increased your expertise as a hobby project designer—using open source tools, applications, and scripts.

Now, you can use the knowledge and skills you acquired to build even more innovative project designs.

# Index

resolution and frame rate, for movement detection 65

webcam installation, testing 62-64

MP3 72

mpg123 34

MSTSC 6

multipart jpeg format (mjpeg) 64

# N

navigate.py
  camera data, analysing 171, 172
  downloading 168-170
  implementing 168
  open loop servo control 170, 171
  steering methodology 170

network bandwidth 72

NOOBS lite Version 1.4.0 9

NOOBS Version 1.4.0 9

NXP PCA9685 I2C chip 131

# O

omxplayer 64

Openbox 23

OpenCV 163

output indicators
  LEDs, driving as 102, 103

# P

Parallax
  URL 128

PC
  remote session, testing from 149

PCA 9685
  about 135
  programming, for driving servo 134

PCA 9685, registers
  ALL_LED 135
  LEDxx 135
  MODE1 135
  PRE_SCALE 135

PCA9685-specific code
  functions 140

PCManFM file manager
  about 28
  root privileges, adding 29-31

Perma-Proto HAT 101

physical switch interface
  adding, to Internet radio 116-119

PiCam
  operation, verifying 50
  URL 42

PiCam camera
  webcam movement detector, combining with 66, 67

picam.sh script
  testing 57, 58

Pi desktop and software configuration
  development environment, updating 24
  performing 23, 24
  screensaver, setting up 25, 26
  session, locking manually 27

Pi, hardware and software networking configuration
  about 18-21
  client reservations, for Ethernet and wireless 22

Pillow
  about 164
  installing 165

PiNoIR 42

pip manager
  installing 164

pip package manager
  installing 164
  URL, for documentation 164

Pi-View HDMI-to-VGA cable 8

playlist file
  designing, for Internet radio 87
  parsing, for Internet radio 88

PLS 72

PortaPow USB Power Monitor V2
  URL 151

potential battery power solutions
  about 152
  Adafruit PowerBoost 500C 153
  Adafruit PowerBoost 1000 Basic 152, 153
  power banks, as alternative mobile power system 154

power
  configuring, for Raspberry Pi 4-6

**Thank you for buying**
# Raspberry Pi Essentials

## About Packt Publishing

Packt, pronounced 'packed', published its first book, *Mastering phpMyAdmin for Effective MySQL Management*, in April 2004, and subsequently continued to specialize in publishing highly focused books on specific technologies and solutions.

Our books and publications share the experiences of your fellow IT professionals in adapting and customizing today's systems, applications, and frameworks. Our solution-based books give you the knowledge and power to customize the software and technologies you're using to get the job done. Packt books are more specific and less general than the IT books you have seen in the past. Our unique business model allows us to bring you more focused information, giving you more of what you need to know, and less of what you don't.

Packt is a modern yet unique publishing company that focuses on producing quality, cutting-edge books for communities of developers, administrators, and newbies alike. For more information, please visit our website at www.packtpub.com.

## About Packt Open Source

In 2010, Packt launched two new brands, Packt Open Source and Packt Enterprise, in order to continue its focus on specialization. This book is part of the Packt Open Source brand, home to books published on software built around open source licenses, and offering information to anybody from advanced developers to budding web designers. The Open Source brand also runs Packt's Open Source Royalty Scheme, by which Packt gives a royalty to each open source project about whose software a book is sold.

## Writing for Packt

We welcome all inquiries from people who are interested in authoring. Book proposals should be sent to author@packtpub.com. If your book idea is still at an early stage and you would like to discuss it first before writing a formal book proposal, then please contact us; one of our commissioning editors will get in touch with you.

We're not just looking for published authors; if you have strong technical skills but no writing experience, our experienced editors can help you develop a writing career, or simply get some additional reward for your expertise.

## Raspberry Pi Cookbook for Python Programmers

ISBN: 978-1-84969-662-3            Paperback: 402 pages

Over 50 easy-to-comprehend tailor-made recipes to get the most out of the Raspberry Pi and unleash its huge potential using Python

1. Install your first operating system, share files over the network, and run programs remotely.

2. Unleash the hidden potential of the Raspberry Pi's powerful Video Core IV graphics processor with your own hardware accelerated 3D graphics.

3. Discover how to create your own electronic circuits to interact with the Raspberry Pi.

## Raspberry Pi Robotic Projects

ISBN: 978-1-84969-432-2            Paperback: 278 pages

Create amazing robotic projects on a shoestring budget

1. Make your projects talk and understand speech with Raspberry Pi.

2. Use standard webcam to make your projects see and enhance vision capabilities.

3. Full of simple, easy-to-understand instructions to bring your Raspberry Pi online for developing robotics projects.

Please check **www.PacktPub.com** for information on our titles

open source
community experience distilled

## Raspberry Pi for Secret Agents

ISBN: 978-1-84969-578-7        Paperback: 152 pages

Turn your Raspberry Pi into your very own secret agent toolbox with this set of exciting projects!

1. Detect an intruder on camera and set off an alarm.

2. Listen in or record conversations from a distance.

3. Find out what the other computers on your network are up to.

4. Unleash your Raspberry Pi on the world.

## Raspberry Pi Server Essentials

ISBN: 978-1-78328-469-6        Paperback: 116 pages

Transform your Raspberry Pi into a server for hosting websites, games, or even your Bitcoin network

1. Unlock the various possibilities of using Raspberry Pi as a server.

2. Configure a media center for your home or sharing with friends.

3. Connect to the Bitcoin network and manage your wallet.

Please check **www.PacktPub.com** for information on our titles

CPSIA information can be obtained
at www.ICGtesting.com
Printed in the USA
BVHW08s0715150918
527610BV00003B/23/P